"IT'S ALL ABOUT FAITH"

Volume 1

Author: Teresa Sheppard

<u>PREFACE</u>

FAITH is the key that unlocks the gate in which your prayers go through.

God inspired me to create this book. I am thankful to the Christians who donated entries. I pray that God will bless them all. My role has been nothing more than typist and project manager. I am honored to work for God. The true "author" is Jesus. The Bible says (Hebrews Chapter 12 Verse 2) *"Looking unto Jesus the author and finisher of our FAITH, who, for the joy was set before him, endured on the cross, despising the shame, and is set down at the right hand of the throne of God."*

Everything in our lives truly is **"ALL ABOUT FAITH".** Through FAITH in our heavenly father Jesus Christ we know that all things are possible. We also know that James 2:5 says this: *"Hearken, my beloved brethren, Hath not God chosen the poor of this world to be rich in FAITH, and heirs of the kingdom which he hath promised to them that love him?"* In this book you will hear from people who love God. You will learn how Jesus Christ through FAITH leads their lives. You may find that this text is not in perfect grammatical form. In fact I will assure you that it is not. Professional editors did not review the text. I reviewed it. My editing skills are remedial at best. It's important that the words of testimony and FAITH are written as given to each person from God. A special effort has also been made to type each scripture from the Bible exactly as it is written. If you look for faults with me or the others who contributed to this book you will find an abundance. That's one of the greatest things about God; He loves us just as we are. You can be certain all who contributed to this book are sinners saved by God's grace. St. John 3:3 *"Jesus answered and said unto him, <u>Verily, verily, I say unto thee, Except a man be born again, he cannot see the kingdom of God.</u>"* Please read and enjoy the inspirational content, bearing in mind it was written in the spirit without regard for writing technique.

CHAPTER 1

SALVATION

(**Ephesians 2:8-9** *For by grace are ye saved through FAITH; and that not of yourselves: it is the gift of God: Not of works, lest any man should boast.*)

Bible School
Beeler, Rebekah - TN

I had gone to Bible school for several years. Each year it was fun. The year I got saved was the best! It was on a Saturday during commencement services. All the families of all the children that attended Bible school that year were there. I was a very shy girl. I never wanted to have attention drawn to me. I listened to the preacher speak about how once you reach the age of accountability if you didn't know Jesus as Saviour and if you hadn't asked him to save then you would die and go to Hell. I had chills before he even spoke a work. The Lord knew that this was the day that I was going to reach the age of accountability. I heard the Lord speak to me. I could feel him. My heart was pounding. My breathing got heavier yet I couldn't move. I was so scared! I couldn't sit still. I was squirming in my seat. My feet wouldn't be still but I couldn't stand. The tears started coming. I started praying before anyone else could even pray with me. It was obvious that I was being dealt with. One of the preachers came to where I was sitting and asked me if I needed him to pray with me. I said yes, but I had already prayed and God had already saved me. I did eventually make it to the front of the church to finish praying. I felt such a calming peace. I knew then and there that if I died I would go to heaven. The very next day Satan started making me doubt my salvation. I began to wonder if I just got caught up in the preaching or in the music. My grandmother was a very spiritual woman. She got to witness me getting saved that night. I called her and told her I was having doubts about my salvation. She began to speak about the Bible and asked me some questions. It was then I realized how quickly Satan will move to try to make even believers try to doubt God. There's been times in my life when I have been out of church, but God has always been there with me and will always be there.

Rebekah left this note for the author: "Thank you for giving me the opportunity to tell people about one of the many things that God has done for me. This is probably the best one because I know without a doubt that when I die I will live forever in a beautiful place where there will be no sorrow or pain." {**Author's Note:** Amen. I couldn't have said it any better. Knowing you are saved is knowing you will spend eternity with Jesus in Heaven and avoid the damnation of Hell. Salvation is certainly the greatest of all God's gifts unto us.}

On My Knees
Beets, Burnis – TN

I was 14 or 15 years old. They was having a revival at Alder Springs Baptist Church. Johnny Ralley was the pastor. He still attends services there today. We walked into the service a big bunch of us. They had a good service that night. It's like you don't know what's going on. One minute I was just sittin' there the next minute I was down on my knees. When I come up from there I was saved and I been saved ever since. This is 2006 and I am 72 years old. {**Author's Note:** I've known Ms. Beets all my life. She is one who has never been afraid to tell it like it is.}

A Few of My Miracles
Bolden, Emily - VA

There's been so many miracles in my life. I could talk from now until eternity, and not get close to telling you about them all.

My first miracle was 30 years ago when God saw fit to let me be part of his kingdom. I got saved! At this time I was raising my three (3) children by myself. I didn't have any money. I went to church regularly. I never had money for gas but God always made a way. I went to church one night praying and crying that there would be gas to go to work the next day. My car was on empty when I went into church and when I came out it had ½ a tank. That had to be God. Another time I was out of Gas. I had no grocery money either. I lived in an old two story house (we had an outside toilet). I laid across the car crying. The Lord spoke to me and told me to go to work. This happened for three (3) days. The third day the phone rang at work. It was for me. It was a friend I hadn't spoke to in a long time. She said 'Emily the Lord has laid it upon my heart to pay you my tithes." It was enough money to buy gas, groceries, and even pay the light bill. I am so thankful to God.

My daughter was about eight (8) years old. She was in a coma. The doctor said she had Toxemia (infection in her blood). The doctor did not think she would live. I was so upset. I went into the waiting room. I met this poorly dressed woman. The woman told me that my little girl was going to be ok. Within a few hours my little girl came out of the coma and was ready to eat. I went back to look for the woman and she was no where to be found. I feel like that woman was an angel. My daughter is now grown and working as a registered nurse.

Many years ago. I had a lump in my left breast. It was so large it went from the nipple to under my arm. The doctor said it did not look good at all. I went to bed praying in the Holy Ghost. When I woke up the next morning it was gone.

I was in a troubled marriage. I would come home from church and my husband would beat me. He was mean to my children. He tried to do bad things to my oldest daughter. The Lord told me one morning (May 3rd) I would be delivered. I questioned God about when it was going to take place. I shouldn't have done that but I did.

You know at 11:45 P.M. I had to get a warrant for him. I came out of the courthouse at around midnight. I never had to worry about that man beating me again.

As the years have went by I've counted on the Lord for everything I needed. I lost a job that I had because I serve God. I didn't know how I'd pay my rent. God gave me a new car, he put it on somebody's heart to give it to me free of charge. I was looking for a job, a woman knew me and trusted me and immediately gave me a job making more money than what I had made before.

I was going to a little church. One night a man came through the door. I loved him the minute he walked through the door. I knew God had sent him to me. I knew I would always love him and I knew he would take care of me. I did not know what the future held, but I knew there was a reason. We started dating and dated for 6 or 8 months. He went and learned to drive a tractor trailer. We corresponded while he was away in Arkansas. (That's where he went to learn how to drive the big trucks) He called me one day and asked what I was doing then next day. I said nothing. He said "Quit your job we are getting married on Friday." That suited me just fine. I went on the road with him. We witnessed to people on the road and I got to see many miracles. The dispatcher from the trucking company would call us to pray for others. We passed out prayer cloths to people all over the United States. People would tell us we had the Holy Ghost. It was the most wonderful time of my life.

We had to come off the truck to take care of my dying mother. God used this time to restore the love I should have had for her. She wasn't good to me during my time of youth. She said she wished I had never been born. God gave me five (5) years to forgive her and learn to love her. She died in 1998.

Me and my husband had a few years to spend time together. Then we got a phone call from social services. His grandchildren were being abused. We went and got them. This was about five (5) years ago. God sent us to take care of those babies so they wouldn't be abused. God let us rescue those children. We've tried to teach them about the goodness of God. Now when we are sick or down and out all three of them will lay there hand on us and pray for us.

God don't trust everybody with his children and all children are his. I am so thankful God let me rescue them. When I was little I had nobody to rescue me.

Billy my oldest one is eleven (11) years old. He is called into the service of God. When Gracie Smallwood's mother died Billy said, "I need to go pray for sister Gracie." We took him to see her. He asked God to heal her broken heart. {**Author's Note**: His prayer really was a blessing Gracie says that she had a heart broken in a million pieces and God did heal it.} He is a miracle from God. He prays all the time. We have a neighbor that died. Three (3) days before she died, he said he couldn't pray for her anymore because God said he was going to take her home in three (3) days. Billy wasn't wrong in three (3) days God did call her home.

The oldest girl Holly has worn glassed all her life. She had her vision checked the other day and now she has 20/20 vision. The Good Lord healed her!

Our van tore up we didn't have no money to buy a new one. I said Lord you know we've got these children. We had stopped and glanced at one at a car lot. I told the Lord we needed something for the children. I said Lord if its meant for us, let it work out. Within ten (10) minutes God worked out a way we could have the very van we looked at to take care of our children. I am so thankful to God for all things. He gave me a wonderful husband and family. Through all these years I've served him. I could never touch all the things he s done. He gives me life everyday and allows me to worship him everyday. The freedom I have in my soul can't be described.

I love the Lord and what he's done and how he saved my soul and set me free from the sins of this world. I can't wait to walk on the streets of gold and thank him. He's always there with me no matter how hard it is to carry the load he helps me. I appreciate this book I know God is in it. God's put a blessing on this tape and the Devil has tried to stop it. I couldn't find a tape recorder I had to go and buy one. I can feel the spirit of God all over this. {**Author's Note:** She sent me her entry on audio cassette. I could feel the spirit of God in the words she spoke.}

I Got It!
Brasher, Courtney - TN

I was born on June 27, 1984. My parents were not attending church at the time although both of them had been raised in church as kids, they had both fallen away. My aunt Sue asked my parents to come to church with her because she had rededicated her life to God and found her church to be very exciting. My parents decided that they would take us: my two brothers and I, and our family also found church very enticing. I was around four at this time. I was raised in church from this time on, when Sunday or Wednesday came along there was no questions as to whether or not we were going to church, it was just what we knew we did on those days. A few years later around the age of 8 or so, we were at church, and my cousin came to me and asked me if I would like to go to the alter; I said yes, and we went. I remember getting up, I remember crying, I remember the preacher, but, I also remember when we left that day my parents asked me to tell my grandmother (we went to her house every Sunday after church). I remember not being very excited to tell her about it. I went from then until a few years later and I never stopped going to church but, I wasn't feeling what everyone else was feeling. On October 20, 1999, I think it was a Wednesday that changed, the message was over; and we were going around shaking hands, well, I didn't make it past the alter, I went to a woman who went to the church and she prayed with me, that day I GOT IT! Not every day is easy, but each night when I lay down, I can count my many blessings. {**Author's Note:** I only met Courtney recently but she has a wonderful spirit about her. She was recently married to a young preacher. I am sure she will be in much need of your prayers for the road ahead.}

How Jesus Changed Me
Chamberlain, Jimmy - TN

I was raised by a strict father, and a firm and very loving mother. I was a good kid (not because I wanted to be, but I was afraid not to be). I was told that I was mature for my age and very well behaved. When I did do wrong; I would worry and fret over it so that my worry would be far worse than the punishment I received from my father. I began to notice this and eventually I over came this fear (which was actually my conscience trying to keep me straight).

In my mid-teens I began to rebel against authority. I would pretend to do right in front of my parents, but behind their backs I did my own thing. And once I began to do wrong more and more and get by with it; my heart grew colder and colder toward others and their feelings. I had a lot of anger and was very vulgar in expressing myself. To become my friend at that time in my life; you had to pass the test of the first impression. Those that I liked when we first met I was nice to. If they said anything or done anything I didn't agree with I would be mean and hateful to them. The farther I went down this wrong road the less I tried to hide my true self. I was so selfish I even argued and nearly fought with my two closest friends. Years later my friends admitted to me that I was so bad (mean and hateful) that they didn't know why they continued to be my friends. I was pretending to have the time of my life, doing my own thing, not a care in this world. But inside I was hurting and I was miserable. I began seeing this girl. Her mom began inviting me to go to church with them. At first I would say maybe, or I might, or someday I will. She always ended her invitation the same way, "We (the church) are praying for you." I couldn't put her off any longer because of her persistence (and the prayers of the church) I began to go to church with them.

So now I was going to church (to please my girlfriend's mom). After a month or so, one Sunday night, the preacher began to preach "Jesus". He preached about his birth, his sin free perfect life, his death on the cross for sin and his resurrection from the dead. And I realized for the first time in my life that "Jesus died for me." The sin that caused the death of the "son of God" was my sin. God showed me that because of the sin in my life, I was going to "Hell" if I died in that condition. The "Holy Spirit" began to tug at my heart. He (the Holy Spirit) began to draw me forward. I resisted at first, I didn't know what to do. I realized I was lost and I knew now that "Jesus died (and God raised him from the dead) to save my soul from Hell."

For about forty-five minutes I stayed still. First I was sitting, then we all were standing and I knew I needed Jesus Christ. I just couldn't move. Then a saint of God came back and hugged me. All she said was "I love you." The next thing I knew I was on my knees at the alter pouring my heart out to God. At that moment, God Saved Me!

That was the summer of 1992, two months after my 18th birthday, and 2 months after I graduated from high school. I wish I could say I've served the Lord ever since that day. But even though he saved me; and forgave all my sins, I still let the things of this world come between God and myself. He never left me, I left him.

I had only been saved four or five months when I fell into temptation. I cheated on my girlfriend, and she left me. I was very sorry for what I had done. I repented of the sin and wanted to continue to worship and serve God at my little church, but, I just couldn't keep going their since my ex-girlfriend was there and dating someone from the church. Then I broke the church covenant (and the principles of God's word). I thought that after a week or two, I would go visit and look for a church I could join. Satan took those two weeks and made it harder and harder for me to go the house of God.

Years later (about 8 years later), thanks to prayers of my mom and dad at their church; the Lord brought me back to the fold. I remember I was working-out of town and I had been gone from home for about three months. At home I had a wife and a six month old baby boy. I was feeling homesick and thru that God began to speak to my heart. He (God) reminded me that because of Jesus He saved me. All at once all the guilt and shame of how I was living my life in sin came upon me. Right then and there in the floor of my motel room through tears and heart felt repentance I begged God to forgive me for turning my back on him.

He forgave me and finally I dedicated my life to my Saviour Jesus Christ. When I came home I started going to the church with mom and dad. The Lord led me to join that church six years ago and four years ago he (God) called me to preach the gospel. God has continued to bless me, my family (now I have two boys) and my church. God's been so good to me that I can't even put it to words. All I can say is "Thank you, Lord."

My prayer for you, who are reading this book, is that you have a similar (blessed) relationship with God through his dear son Jesus

Christ. If so we can praise him together. If not seek Jesus while he is near; remember, whosoever shall call upon the name of the Lord (Jesus) shall be saved. {**Author's Note:** I've known Jimmy for years and I never thought he was that bad to be around. He brought out something interesting though, once you are saved it's a lot easier to see your own faults. The Bible teaches us that our righteous is of filthy rags. I guess realizing where we ourselves fail and come short helps us from being judgmental. The Preacher from our little church set a mirror out in front of the alter. I think his point was before you blame others for the condition of the church always start with the person in the mirror.}

I Thought but Now I Know
Chamberlain, Julie – TN

I am Julie Chamberlain and this is my testimony. I got saved – or so I thought – when I was a child. Looking back I just asked to be saved because everyone else did. It doesn't work that way. I eventually got out of church and didn't go back until I was older. I kept letting Satan convince me that I was saved.

While I was out of church I got married and had a child. My mother-in-law kept asking us to church. We started going to her church and my husband decided to join the church. I got up to join the church because my husband did. I knew something wasn't right. On a Sunday morning a man we go to church with got saved. I really knew that something was wrong. I knew I wasn't saved! The bad thing is I let Satan make me believe I would be embarrassed because I had just asked to join. I let pride get in my way. I left church that day lost. I tried to put on a happy face. I got very afraid and started crying al the way home. I cried all the way back to church that night.

I was so afraid I would die knowing that I was lost. Thank the Lord when I got to church the Lord was still calling me. I was trying to wait until the service started but, I couldn't wait. I had to get up. I went to the preacher and told him I needed to get saved. We went to the alter together and I asked the Lord to save me! I am so glad the Lord was still calling me. I couldn't stand the thought of going on any longer knowing that I was lost. {**Author's Note**: Julie is a wonderful and growing Christian.}

My Walk With Christ
Corum, Jeanette

The Lord has been so good throughout the years. He has never failed to watch out for us even when we were not living like we should.

I was saved at the age of twelve (12). I was at church more than at home. When I got married Cecil and I got out of church a while. I know even during these times God's hand was still on my life. God didn't let me rest until I was back in church. I had my children in church so they could hear his word. Just being in church doesn't mean a thing if you are not sold out to God. God has to be the love of your life. I pray daily that he will be the most important thing in my life and that I will be a vessel that he can use.

In his word God said that he would provide for all our needs. He has always provided for us. In 1985 my husband had surgery on his ankle. He was in a cast for six (6) months. I didn't work and he was out of months eight (8) months total. I started making teddy bears. They had a half moon in their chest and I cross stitched "Jesus Loves You" on them. I carried them every went and God did the rest. We lived on the sales of the bears during that eight (8) months. Our bills were paid and we never did without food. When Cecil went back to work the sales stopped. God is so FAITHful to his word! I thank you Lord for your word and your FAITHfulness!

In 1989 my husband again had o be out of work. Cecil fell on the job and hurt his back. He couldn't get up or around for months without help. For eighteen (18) months he was in therapy and out of work for three (3) years. During the first several months we were working with workers compensation and getting payments. He started getting checks after about five weeks, but they were small. Again, my God took care of us. We started making calendars out of plastic canvas. We had so many orders that we would get up around 06:00 A.M. in the morning and start work on them until around 11:00 P.M. When we got back pay from workers compensation and an insurance policy he had the sales slowed down. You do the best you can do and God will do the rest. God is always FAITHful. To God be the glory!

When you feel a need from within your spirit to pray don't dismiss it! You never know whose life is depending on your prayer. I believe with all my heart that the Lord will impress on us to lift someone up in prayer and that he will act on our prayers.

Let me tell you why I know this is true. I learned this lesson in September of 2000. Our daughter, her husband, and infant were stationed at Fort Brag in North Carolina. They were getting transferred to Alaska. Their belongings had been packed and loaded. They were going to come home (Tennessee) and spend two (2) weeks with family before leaving. On September 25, 2000 they finished up in North Carolina and started to Tennessee. That morning I felt that I should call and tell them to wait a while until the rain let up before starting out. I didn't call. About 05:15 that afternoon I felt a strong feeling to pray. I prayed that the Lord would put his hand of protection on whomever he was wanting me to pray for. I didn't know who it was, but I knew I needed to pray. I prayed he would go before them and that he would put a wall around about them. Above and below. At the same time my oldest daughter had the same feeling. My middle daughter was on her way to church and she had the same feeling. At 05:15 P.M. the three (3) of us were all praying for someone. We didn't know whom, but we were all praying.

Around 05:25 P.M. my youngest daughter was in a car accident. A drunk driver in a Dodge Ram Pickup ran a stop sign and hit their Honda. The truck came up on their hood. My daughter said that the truck was headed for their windshield and all of a sudden it was like a hand stopped the truck and pushed it back off the car. I think it was the hand of God. My son-in-law was driving. He hit the wheel and only had bruises. The infant was unharmed. My daughter was hurt. She had three (3) broken ribs, a broken arm, her lungs collapsed, she had a cut on her spleen, and a lot of bruises. They took her to the hospital. The doctor from the hospital called us around 06:00 P.M. that evening. We told the church what had happened and they prayed for us. We left to go be with our daughter. We left in the clothes we had on and had very little money. When we got to the hospital we found out that she would be there at least a week. Our God is so

17

good. We were able to keep the baby in the waiting room. They brought a baby bed in for us and milk for his bottle. Cecil sang in a church that found out about the wreck. The church came and prayed with our daughter. The church put us up in a motel for ten (10) days and brought us $200.00 for meals while we were there. Again our Lord takes care of his children. He watched over our daughter and healed her body. We brought her home to stay with us while she was recovering. My daughter and her family stayed with us for four (4) months. They did not want to go to Alaska and we did not want them to go. Little did we know God would use this thing to keep them from going. God did not do this, but God allowed it to happened. Somewhere the Bible says all things work to t he good for them that love the Lord. Throughout this a lot of people saw God work in so many different ways. Thank you Lord for watching over this family and for your protection over them. Thank you for answering our prayers.

There's many more stories I could tell, but this is a little bit of my walk with Jesus. {**Author's Note**: Jeanette really blessed my heart. She is strong in her FAITH and know what God can and will do. Those that love God must love him everyday and submit to him everything. God will take care of every detail and aspect of our lives as long as we will let him.}

Whosoever Will
Dyer, Amy – TN

Hello, my name is Amy. I am from Tennessee. I would like to share my testimony. I was raised in and out of different churches when I was a child. My mom and dad divorced when I was five (5) years old. My dad was in and out of my life. Mostly out. No, I'm not looking for pity. I know there are people who have it worse. I do feel like the Lord is wanting me to share my testimony to as many people as I can. The Bible tells us in James 4:14 *"Whereas ye know not what shall be on the morrow; For what is your life? It is even a vapor, that appearath for a little time, and then vanisheth away."*

I was molested when I was nine (9) years old by my step grand-father. I had to have counseling when I was a child. I had a violent temper. I would destroy things when I got mad. That lasted into my teenage years and continued to get worse. I was saved when I was ten (10) at an old fashioned church. Getting saved was the best thing that ever happened to me! That is something I will never forget. After I was saved we were in and out of church. My step dad and I didn't get along. He never abused me, but he was too strict. He was raised in a real strict home.

I got married when I was twenty (20) years old. I met my husband at the church I belonged to. I prayed since I was about thirteen (13) that God would lead me to the one he would have me be with. I dated off an on but, nothing seemed to click. Every time I would start to fall for someone I would pray and God would show me somehow that they weren't the one. When I met my husband I prayed and it fell into place. That is the way God wanted it. The weekend of our honeymoon my husband was voted in as pastor of a little Missionary Baptist Church.

I was diagnosed with a chemical imbalance. They also said that I was Bipolar Type 2. I prayed and asked God what to do. I was getting worse. I was put in the hospital on the mental health floor. I questioned God. The is the hardest thing I have ever went through. I thought "God, am I doing something wrong? Am I being punished for something?" The Lord revealed to me through different people and my church family that there was a reason for it. The reason was to help others spiritually and naturally. I look back now and although it seemed like my longest trial, My Lord and Saviour never left me.

Hebrews 13:6 *"So we may boldly say, the Lord is my helper, and I will not fear what man shall do unto me."* God showed me that when you're truly saved and born again that it is forever. I never thought I would have a normal life. I am sitting here now watching cartoons with my little boy. I also have my drivers license. I didn't get them until I was twenty-one (21) years old.

Life still happens. I still have trials and tribulations and I will until the good Lord calls me home. God also led me to the right doctors and medication for my nerves. I know what you are thinking "Oh my gosh you are a Christian and you're on medicine?" Well I had to struggle with that too! I didn't want to attempt on doing anything without asking God to lead and guide me. I'm still human. I need the Lord everyday. I could not and would not want to try to live without him. There is nothing that could ever compare to knowing that you have eternal salvation. Salvation that only God can give you through his son, Jesus Christ. In the holy word of God St. John 3:3 says "***Jesus answered and said unto him, <u>verily, verily I say unto thee, except a man be born again, he cannot see the kingdom of God</u>.***"

No matter who you are or what you've done I want you to know Jesus loves you! In John 3:16-17 "<u>***For God so loved the world, that he gave his only begotten son, that whosoever believeth in him, should not perish, but have everlasting life. For God sent not his son into the world to condemn the world; but that the world through him might be saved.***</u>" I am going to list some scripture I'd like for you to read for yourself. John 14:6, Hebrews 11:1, John 14:27, Romans 10:13-17, Matthew 7:7, and Matthew 6:33. {**Author's Note**: Amy has received a miracle from God. You would never know by talking to her that she has the conditions mentioned in her testimony. God must surely dwell within her heart.}

God is Concerned with Our Soul
Dyer, Jason Rev. – TN

I would like to give my greatest testimony. My name is Jason Dyer. I am twenty-nine (29) years old, married, the father of one (1), and the pastor of a church. I believe nothing is impossible with God. I also believe (Spiritual and Physical) God is able to heal on all accounts. I believe this will all my heart because of the word of God.

I have read that God is more concerned with our soul than with our flesh. If a person lived to be a hundred years old, but died lost without Christ (Even if they'd been healthy all those years) it would not compare to eternity. Heaven is forever and Hell is also. God gave his son for ransom to mankind that they might be saved through his life changing blood. Jesus did this so that we could escape the awful place called Hell. That is why I know God is concerned more about the soul than the flesh. The soul will live forever. We will all either live forever with God (Heaven) or forever separated from God (Hell).

I could testify of the many times God healed my physical body. I praise God for the times he has healed me. I know without a doubt that he has. The physical healing would be worth nothing if I did not know Jesus as my personal Saviour.

The main thing is my soul. My soul has been healed and no matter what happens to me physically I'm ready to meet and live with God forever! Praise the name of Jesus. I once was blind, lame, and diseased spiritually in my soul. I met Jesus and he made me whole and complete. Jesus gave me peace and joy that money can not buy.

When I was eleven (11) years old in the summer of 1988 I came to the understanding that I was lost. I was at my grandparents house. They were listening to the gospel station on the radio. A preacher was preaching the word of God. His message was to the lost and it convicted me. I never realized in my life that I was a sinner lost without God. That day God showed me that I was lost. God started dealing with my heart. I started asking questions. I was seeking and could not sleep at night. I was afraid I would die and I knew I would go to Hell. There was a lot of people praying for me. Nobody could save me but Jesus and Nobody could ask Jesus to save me but me. I was under the conviction of the Holy Spirit for two (2) weeks. They were having a revival at church that week and I got saved! The preacher was preaching the love of Jesus. The Lord spoke to me and said now is the time to come. They gave the alter call and Jesus drew me with his spirit to the alter. I got up on my own and went to accept Jesus. I have never been the same since that day. I really did not even know what to say with my lips, but Jesus knew what I was wanting in my heart. Jesus forgave me that night. I became a new creature in Christ. I was a born again Christian! I still am today. I did not work for the gift of grace that night. I simply believed on Jesus and accepted that gift. I'm not living right to get salvation. I'm living right because I have salvation. God Bless you all! {**Author's Note**: Jason is my pastor. I think his main goal with the church is seeing the lost find their way to an alter of salvation.}

Saved

Gibson, Edna – TN

I am saved! {**Author's Note**: Edna is a wonderful woman.}

God Changed Me

Hensley, Leroy - TN

My name is Leroy Hensley, I am 65 years old. My testimony is like a lot of other peoples. I was raised up in church and taught about Jesus. I never really thought too much about dying or where I would go when I died, until I got a whole lot older. My wife and I have been married for 40 years. We have been in and out of church several times. I thought at one time I got saved but I found out later that I wasn't. The difference from then and now this time there is no doubt. God took a man named Leroy and made a different person out of me. All I used to think about was going out on the weekend and drinking and playing music with the guys. Now my life has made a complete turn a round. It's amazing what God can do with your life if you will just ask him to forgive you of your sins and really mean it. There's no doubt in my mind he will save you and your life will never be the same.

I've been a Christian since 1998 and I think back of all the years and all the heartache I've put my family through. I have a wonderful wife and three wonderful sons. My prayer is to live to see my sons accept Jesus and live for him. They are just like I was, thinking they are going to live forever (forever in the fleshly sense). I wish they could understand this old world has nothing compared to knowing that you can live in Heaven with Jesus. You can have everlasting life with our Lord and Saviour Jesus Christ. That's the reason I want to see all my family saved. This is my testimony. Without Jesus we have nothing but with him we have everything. I was lost, but now I'm found. God Bless You. {**Author's Note**: I am well acquainted with Mr. Hensley's story. He gave you a brief summary, but I can assure you the more you learn about his testimony the more you'll realize what a blessing he is.}

What God will Do.
Hodge, Jackie Richard – TN
(Jackie Richard Hodge-is an Award Winning Gospel Singer, Songwriter Columnist and Poet)

This story is to show others what God will do if you are obedient. Remember this word "Obedient." I've wanted to sing as long as I can remember. My mother would sing country and gospel songs around the house, as far back as I can remember. I was always a music lover, I was told; Before I could walk or talk, Mom would turn on music on the radio, they would hold me up and my little legs would go with the music. As I got older I sang along with the country singers on the radio, with singers like Hank Williams Senior, The Chuckwagon Gang and singers on the Mid Day Merry Go Round on WNOX out of Knoxville, Tennessee. In the summer we would gather with neighbors and friends on the front porch. Mom would play the guitar and we would sing. It would be a mixture of gospel and country music. As I entered into my teen years, Rock and Roll was the big thing ; By this time we had moved up north to Illinois, as Mom was ill, and we went to live with my older brother Bob and his wife Loretta. Dad died when I was 9 years old, and Mom was having a hard time. But that's another story. As a teenager, I wanted to be a Rock singer. At 16, I was given the opportunity to record a love song; I took the time to learn the song. It was a beautiful song, but I thought it would cramp my style, so I turned it down. Keep in mind, God had a plan for me. I was being molded along the way for bigger and better work for Him.

At 17 I got saved, I worked for the Lord for about a year. A word to those leading and rearing young Christians, choose carefully what you say to them. I will not go into detail at this time but a minister I believed in caused me to leave the Church with a statement he made.

A few years passed and I began to sing from time to time in night clubs and bars. but never went anywhere with my music. As years came and went I spent time talking with God, most of the time when something went wrong and I needed His help, and that was quite often. Years passed, and I lost business after business, my home and finally my family. I had not turned my back on God, but I wasn't being obedient to God. There is that word again "Obedient." Remember this powerful word.

I wandered around from here to there for a while then decided to return to Tennessee, after loosing everything I owned and Loved; I had been striped like Job. In 1992, I married a woman that had sung Gospel music for 35 years. In 1993, going through the mountains on I-40 east on our way to visit my brother in-law in North Carolina. I popped in a gospel tape of the McKamey's. "Under His Feet" was playing and the tears began to stream down my face. The Spirit was so strong in the car that day. You needed to have been there and experienced what I felt that day to know what I mean. I gave my life back to God.

When we returned from North Carolina, my wife Dela and I began to sing in churches around our area. I bought a guitar and Dela taught me a few cords, and I would sing with the guitar. Sometimes I would play, but most of the time Dela would play when we sang. Well, Satan got upset; he had lost me again and he thought he could get me back. "Wrong"! I'm getting ahead of my story. In 1994 I had a heart attack. With a bad heart, asthma and emphysema I am now on disability. My wife Dela became very sick with cirrhosis of the liver. She got worse and worse. The last 2 years were the worst, as at times she didn't know how to feed herself; Sometimes she would ask me how to go to sleep and other things. If you have never dealt with someone with this type of disease it is hard for me to explain. Dela finally went into a coma and passed away; I went through a very bad time, depression and such. I didn't know what I was going to do. But, I felt it was time I took control and get back into life.

I asked a lady friend, Linda, to have dinner and conversation with me. This was part of Gods plan for me and her, as we fell in love that night as no other two people have ever fell in love. And we got married within 6 months April of 1999. But I'm a little ahead of my story. God had been telling me for about 4 years to stop smoking cigarettes. He had a job for me and that job was to sing for him; In order to do a good job it required me to stop smoking as I had smoked since I was 13 years old,. I have asthma and emphysema. I had said several times "Lord take away the craving for cigarettes." You know this is not what God was looking for. Quitting smoking was very difficult for me. In January of 2000, a friend of mine Dillard Craig said he had quit smoking. I asked him how he did it. He said he had the flu and every time he would try to smoke it would make him sick. As I was driving home from his house that night. I began to talk to God, I said "God, have these cigarettes make me sick so I don't want them." My dear friends, be very careful what and how you ask God to do something. Within a week I was in the hospital dying with my asthma and emphysema, But the night before I went into the Hospital I told God I would not smoke anymore. I was obedient and have stayed obedient. That is what God wants from us.

When I showed the Lord I could be obedient let me tell you all that has happened to me in a short 2 years: I have won 16 National awards with the Tennessee Country Music Association, Gospel Division. I have won 9 International awards with the North American country Music Association, Gospel Division. I came in third in Ed McMahon's, Christmas Star Search. I have toured four states, been on several TV and Radio programs. I have my own radio program Syndicated World wide out of Sevierville, Tennessee., I have been given three Editors Choice Award with the International Library of Poetry. My poetry was chosen for publishing in the "Incandescent Jungle" by the International Library of Poetry. They chose my poem "A Star Was Born" to be put on a compilation album called "Sound Of Poetry". They have published 15 of my poems on CD called "Visions". I have been invited to go to Disney World in Florida to read my poetry and to receive the Poetry of Merit Award and I have been nominated for International Poet Of The Year. Published with Noble House of London, Paris & New York and American Poets. I have 7 CD's and have written 4 of the songs on these CD's. I have written over 200 poems and I have other songs which do not have music to them yet. March 11 2005 I received "Who's Who In Poetry " from the International Library of Poetry and my poem "A Talk With Jesus" is the first poem in the book. I received Christmas Album of the year March 13, 2005, for "Happy Holidays". This award was with North America Country Music Association International. As you can see, God has been good to me. This what God will do for you, too, if you are simply obedient to his wishes. Put him first in your life and he will use you for his work. Just let him. Stay In Gods

Care. {**Author's Note**: This testimony is proof of FAITH, not only the testimony itself, but the way I received it. I was online looking for a website for one of my favorite gospel groups. By God's Grace I stumbled upon Mr. Hodges website. I knew when it appeared in my search results it wasn't the website I was looking for, but I felt that still small voice bidding me to check it out. I did and his testimony was posted on the front page! It touched my heart. I immediately emailed him and asked if I could enter the testimony in this book. Within a matter of hours he not only gave me permission to use the testimony, but sent other entries as well. What a blessing! God lives within us is presence is always there. This should be a reminder to listen closely to what he's trying to tell us. For more information on Mr. Hodge and his works please see his name under the special recognition section in Chapter 6.}

When I Got Saved
Johnson, Rachel Clark - VA

The I got saved in the month of September the year was 1977. I do not remember the day of the month. I know it was on a Thursday. My dad was a preacher and he held revivals everywhere. His name was Bob Clark. This particular two weeks he was in revival at Collins Chapel Church.

My dad always fasted and prayed through revivals. The Devil didn't like it at all. The car had torn up the first week of the revival and I had broken my glasses. We lived in the Klondike in Stickleyville. My dad had to hitchhike to church and to work. We had to stay home and not go with him unless someone came to take us.

My dad always went to the woods to pray. You could hear him everywhere. The sound would carry with the wind.

One day I had butterflies in my stomach the whole day. I didn't know why. It was Thursday and someone came and took us to church. There was my two brothers, my sister, my mom, my dad, and me. I remember the air was cool. At the church there was a lot of singing and then my dad preached. He gave an alter call. I still had the butterflies. I was also crying and my heart felt like it was going to burst. I ran to the alter and fell down on my knees to pray for God to forgive me of my sins and to come into my heart. I felt a lot better after that.

I went to school the next day. Some of my friends asked me what I did last night. They knew my dad was a preacher and we went to church a lot. I told them I got saved at church. They said "saved from what?" I told them from sin and that if I died I was going to Heaven and I did not have to be afraid. I was ten years old then. I am now thirty-eight and still praising and serving the Lord. I was the only one saved during this two week revival. My dad said it was worth every step he walked to see one person saved. God Bless You! {**Author's Note**: You can feel the sincerity in her testimony. I wonder if her dad is still alive and preaching. I sure would like to hear a man like that preach.}

Life Lessons
Peir, Paulette - TN

Growing up we were in church on Sundays and Wednesdays. At age 16 I met a visiting preacher holding revival at our church. I'd accepted Jesus as my personal Saviour. I wanted to know and learn all I could about one who'd love me so much to die for my sins. This led to me wanting to go to church every time the doors were open. This visiting preacher had set up a church in a nearby town and would send his niece around the area for those who needed a ride. I'd go every chance I was allowed. The services had no curtain ending - sometimes we'd be there until 11 P.M. or 12 A.M. I no longer wanted to go to our little church, but this one. When it began to interfere with school the next day my Mama had to restrict my going. When I'd miss this church's services the "preacher" asked why and I told him. This led to him telling me when I turned 17 (in this state) I'd be legal and able to make my own choices – he'd quoted scripture to justify what he said. I wanted more than anything to serve the Lord. So much so I became blinded to the deceit and lies that would soon follow.

When I turned 17(with the "preachers help") I got a summer job in the town where the preacher's church was. I told my Mama I was going to go stay with my older sister, who lived in the same town I worked in. But not so, it was set up for the "preachers" niece to pick me up after work and I went to live with her and her 3 girls. The following day at work my Mama called her heart breaking as her voice over the phone broke thru her tears. She was questioning me. I could never bare to hear my Mama cry and so followed my tears and inability to speak. This call didn't change anything. I'd visit home once in awhile.

A new house was being built and my last visit I recall as Mama and I walked over the foundation she told me, she had the feeling she'd not get to live in it long. What was I to reply to that?

One night I went to revival about an hour away from home. The services were cut short and we were all to go over to one of the member's house. I remember having my overnight bag with me. I always carried an 8x10 photo frame which housed pictures of all my family members. I went on outside with the other kids/teens to talk and play. The grown-ups went in to talk.

Then I was called inside. My thoughts – they wanted to pray for me. They told me to sit down. I recall it was a rocking chair. I sat in it. Then it was beyond description except I felt what kind of cruel joke was this! Why are they doing this to me! The words came, "your mom has been in a wreck" She and my little brother were dead. Once of your sister's was with her and she's alive. As each word came so were the questions. The people are crazy! Before they'd finished, I jumped up and ran out to the vehicle and gathered the picture and began hysterically telling them to take me home! I want to go home! The drive seemed more like one long night.

They did not take me home – not to my home – but to theirs. The "preacher" and his wife, and took me inside telling me I had to "calm down, God's children do no act like this", then proceeded to give me some pills. Questions filtered thru the grief and pain. What? Why? – God's children needed no pills! But I seen the pills as the only way to get them to take me home.

I was numb when we finally arrived at my parents house. I stood between the "preacher" and his wife at the front door of the less than 3 months old new house. I recall seeing my Dad sitting at the end of the table and other brothers and sisters sitting and standing around the words "Mama's dead, and so is Dale & Kathy" coming thru a room of grief – then the "preachers" words "I think she ought to stay wit us" and my Dad's gentle nod of his head and words filled with tears "whatever you think" We were gone! I was still numb. Thru it all I recall going to the church where their bodies were brought, going to the caskets, and who I saw there did not resemble my Mama, brother, and sister I refused to accept it.

As time went on I remained with the church I'd left home for. Within a few months I got married. Within a year of being married I was told "I never loved you" again heartache. If this was love, I wanted no part of it. We were living in a warehouse at the "preacher's" place. I quickly recalled the pills and went in their house and got the pills from the bathroom cabinet. I locked the door and took the pills.

I awoke in the hospital with my Dad and oldest sister over me. Then came the words I never had thought to be so welcome. "You are coming home with us!"

A short time after that church (the one I'd left home for) split up. The "preacher" began moving young girls and women into his home. His wife left and the preacher began living in Old Testament ways, of more that one wife, concubines, and handmaids. It took years but I began to see Mama knew there was something just not right with this church and this preacher, but could not tell me why she no longer wanted me going there, Just that I shouldn't go so much. It took loosing them, (My mom was 43, my brother was 3 and my sister was15) to open my eyes.

{**Author's Note**: I didn't really know how to think or feel when I first read this. I read it over several times and then found this scripture – Matthew 7:15-20 *Beware of false prophets, which come to you in sheep's clothing, but inwardly they are ravening wolves. Ye shall know them by their fruits; Do men gather grapes of thorns or figs of thistles? Even so every good tree bringeth forth good fruit; but a corrupt tree bringeth forth evil fruit. A good tree cannot bring forth evil fruit, neither can a corrupt tree bring forth good fruit. Every tree that bringeth not forth good fruit is hewn down, and cast into the fire. Wherefore, by their fruits ye shall know them.* Not everyone that claims to be "preacher" has been called by God. If you have the FAITH and you pray you will know he whom God has called. The spirit and fruit of the man will bear witness of itself. }

Why Not Tonight?
Pelfrey, Barbara Profitt – TN

I got saved in 1953, when I was 12 years old. My family went to a revival at Riverview Baptist Church. I don't remember the date or the day of the week. It seemed like the preacher was talking about me and my heart felt like it would burst out of my chest. I was sitting in the back f the church. I saw my grandmother Cordelia coming down the aisle toward me I thought. The song was "Why not tonight" The preacher was giving an alter call. I met my grandmother half-way down the aisle and I went to the alter. I poured my heart out praying. I wasn't going to get up 'til I felt something. A bright light came down on me; a nearly blinding light covered me. I came up shouting all over the church. Something I never understood before. My getting saved brought my brother Buddy up to the alter and was saved, that night! We both were baptized in Bull Run Creek (Powell, TN), which is now covered by Melton Hill Lake. {**Author's Note**: This is yet another of my grandmothers. This is the first time I had the opportunity to hear her testimony.}

A Special Night At Bible School
Pelfrey, Charlene –TN

I was saved when I was 12 years old. I went to Bible school at Hines Creek Baptist Church. Every night my Bible teacher talked to us about getting saved. Thursday night after I left church I asked God to save me Friday at church. When Friday came I didn't want to go, but my mother made me. She (my mother) actually had to push me out of the car when we got there. I got saved that night. I thank God he saved me and gave me a mother that cared enough to make me go {**Author's Note**: This is my mom. I always knew she had the FAITH. I remember her reading Bible stories to us as kids. It's funny because in all these years this is the first time I ask her what happened the night she got saved.}

God Takes Away All Doubt
Pelfrey, Darrell - TN

I was 9 years old, in the 4th grade when I was saved. Being a young boy and loving the outdoors I knew there where something great about this earth. I knew there was a God before I was saved. I prayed with my mom at times when I was younger than nine. I was going to Bible school at Riverview Baptist Church in Claxton, TN. Our teacher ask us to pray with her and ask us if any of us wanted to be saved or felt like we needed to be. Well it was bothering me before that day, and when I prayed Lord to save me, God came into my heart, and I knew I would never be the same again, I grew up and many years later I married a beautiful lady named Charlene another gift from God. She went to church all her life. After we were married we were in church one night and I doubted my salvation, my heart was pounding, I went to the alter, but when I prayed the Lord showed me that little church when I was 9 years old in the basement at Bible school. That was where he saved my soul and paid a great price for a little boy who will never forget what he's done for me. {**Author's Note**: This is my daddy. It's the first time I'd heard his testimony. I am very thankful he found his way back to God.}

By Myself
Pelfrey, Josh – TN

A couple of years ago I went to a gospel crusade at my school. My parents are Christians so they signed the permission slip for me to go. During the service a bunch of my buddies got up and went to the alter. I wanted to go, but I couldn't. When they got done another alter all was given. This time I knew I had to go. I went all by myself. When I came up from there I knew I was saved. {**Author's Note**: Josh is my little brother and he is very shy. For him to get up alone if front of all those people it had to be God.}

Don't Be Deceived
Rose, Arlene – TN

When I was twelve (12) years old I joined a church and they didn't teach you had to be saved to go to Heaven. According to them if you joined their church you was o.k. I went to church for years thinking I was saved. People would talk about when they got saved and I didn't understand what they were talking about. I knew I had never had that feeling. I went to church all the time. I got married and still went to that same church all the time. I sang in the quartet and with my family. When my youngest daughter was about five (5) years old we started going to another church. I knew then I had not been saved. My life was miserable! One special Sunday morning at this church I had a heavy load upon my shoulders. There was a visiting preacher at the church. I was asking Jesus please let that preacher say something that would let me know for sure if I was saved. He come back where I was setting and ask me are you saved? I told him I didn't know. He said if you don't know then you haven't been saved! I went to the alter. The church prayed with me and I got saved! I'll never forget the day I got saved! I can go to the place where the Lord saved me. I thank God for saving my soul and for his many blessings. I've been saved now for thirty-four (34) years. {**Author's Note**: Arlene is a beautiful woman both in the Godly and the worldly since. She loves to sing and is very talented with it.}

A Living Testimony
Sheppard, Teresa –TN

I believe that our lives are a living testimony. I want to tell you I've done millions of good deeds and never failed my God. I want to tell you that, but I can't because that's the exact opposite of the truth. I feel impressed by the spirit to give this account of my life. I'm not proud of my sins, but I am willing to confess them if it will help just one soul. If any of you want God in your lives, but still can't let go of your worldly pleasures, I think you will really identify with my story.

I am saved! I am born again! I am a child of God! I was around 13 when I came to know Jesus Christ. I was having trouble sleeping at night. I'd wondered what would happen to me if I died. I was so scared, but I never told a soul. We went to a revival with my aunt (I think it was a Sunday night). I remember the dress I was wearing, I remember the name of the church, I remember the hard wooden pews, I remember the preacher, I remember the sermon about Hell, I remember feeling like every word he said was for me and only me, and I remember the alter call. I took the first step -scared to death to move and more afraid not to. I believe he saved me when I took that first step. I was saved by the Grace of God. I am eternally thankful for the gift I received that night.

My FAITH was strong. Every time I got into trouble I knew I could pray and the Lord would help me. Too bad that's the only time I prayed. (Not counting those half-hearted bedtime prayers.)

I entered high school. I never drank, I never smoked, never stopped going to church, I never got in with the "wrong" crowds, I never failed a class, and I never used drugs. The worst thing I did was start a few fights. They were usually about my boyfriend. I sure did love him. In fact I loved him a lot more than I loved God. I prayed a lot about him. I prayed because I didn't want to loose him. He and I went to church together for a while and it was great. No, not because he might be a good solider and work for God. I thought it was great because when he was at church I didn't have to worry about what he might be doing without me. He wasn't just any guy he was 18 and the whole world revolved around him! It's not easy for a 15 year old to hang on to an "older" man. My parent's made the situation more impossible because they were too strict. No, not once did they let us spend the night together. They never even let me stay out past 11:00 p.m. It was my parents fault if he went out with other girls. Who could blame him? He shouldn't have to suffer because of my parents! What an outrage! My parent's even went as far to tell me that a boy that age would have "things" on his mind. They told me I should date someone my own age. I let them know real quick that I was not going to stop seeing him. I would have done anything to keep him and they knew it. The nerve of my parents! The year I started dating him they (the parents) bought me a Bible for my birthday. I thought it was a pretty stupid gift, but looking back it's probably the best gift I've ever gotten. I know what my parents were afraid of. They thought I'd be having sex. They were right! The Bible does say that your husband should be your first. I knew what the Bible said, but I loved him! Besides I knew I was going to marry him, which would mean that my husband was my first. Who cared what order they happened in? I wasn't committing any sin. (If the flesh wants something bad enough it's easy to justify sin. Give it any justification you want it is still sin.) I did marry the boyfriend when I was 17 years old. I promised God if he would let me marry this boy that we would serve him. We did not! I thought it was going to be the fairy tale life. Not much later when we were getting divorced the fairy tale ended. I thought I would die! Part of me did die. I prayed the Lord would give him back to me. See I never forget how to call on the Lord when I was in trouble. This time God said no. My divorce did go through. I was a teenager and divorced! I should have repented my sins. I should have turned to God, but I didn't. I sought comfort in the world.

I needed to have fun. I deserved it! I didn't have many friends (1 actually) because I didn't care about anyone or anything except the "x". My only friend was ready for fun too! We went to a local pool hall. There we met lots of other "new friends". I was so depressed the first time I went there. One of the older boys offered to buy me some drinks, so I said "ok". That's the first time I ever drank! My new friends (who were acquaintances for years through the "x") made sure I got home safely. I felt so guilty the next day. I said "I'll never drink again!" I wasn't living close to God, but getting drunk just didn't feel right. I really came to trust my new friends. (No, not God my friends) The new friends were family to me. We had lots of fun. We hang out together almost every day for what seemed like a long time.

I'd loved my new friends (the guys), but one night me and the girls went to Gatlinburg. We were there to flirt with boys and just have some fun. No drinking - no drugs just some fun. That night I met this man. He was 6'6" tall and handsome. He had an awesome car and a pretty smile. He really seemed to like me. I gave him my number, and he called me the very next day. I was so excited. I had my first date with him that night. He was such a gentleman. I mean really a gentlemen. We watched a movie and he very gently put his arm around me. That's the only move he made! Wow, I sure was impressed with him. As time went by I moved in with him. I know it wasn't a "Christian-like" thing to do. It was ok though, see my husband had been my first, me and this guy were both divorced so even if we'd gotten married lots of preachers would still called it adultery, besides I knew I was saved, and this just wasn't a time to be thinking about religion. I knew I was living in sin and it bothered me a little, but I thought that was better than jumping back into a marriage & getting divorced again. Nope, I wasn't going to put myself through that again. I knew I couldn't marry him anyway.

NO, he didn't drink (see I wouldn't date a guy who drank), he didn't use drugs and he was always good to me. I did love him, but I wasn't completely over my first. This guy he knew that and was cool about it. He was older though, must have been at least 15 years older than me. That's not why I couldn't marry him; I couldn't marry him because .... I'll just say it was because of his choice in careers. I knew it wouldn't be "Christian-like" to marry a man who lived this lifestyle. Somehow I could justify living with him, but not marriage. Marriage would have been wrong! (I will say again, Give it any justification you want it's still sin and I knew it.) My relationship with him eventually ended. We ended things on good terms. I just hope and pray he gets his heart right with God, before it's too late.

I started going to night clubs. It's ok though, see I don't drink at night clubs and I don't go home with men. Going home with men and drinking at the night clubs would be dangerous and wouldn't be "Christian-like". It was ok to go, because I wasn't participating in the activities. I did drink, but not at clubs. I drank at restaurants. You know…just a social drink with the girls, a drink while we bet on ball games or talked about girl things. No men, no drugs, just a safe relaxing social drink with the girls. (This is when God really started to deal with me.) I had an argument with my mom one Sunday night. Sunday's were a big night at one of my favorite spots. After church I stopped at my mom's to change into my club clothes. She said "You just went to church and now you are going to a bar!" I said "No, mother, I am going to a club" She said "It's the same thing, you know better than that!" I said "I know the Bible says to avoid drunkenness, but I don't remember it saying not to have fun!" Her comeback "You can't go down a chimney without getting a little suet on you!" I left. What did she know? That night I had no fun what-so-ever! I was there in body but not in spirit. Clubs just weren't as much fun once God started dealing with me. It wasn't long after that I quit going to church, but I began to read my Bible. Remember that Bible I got for my birthday. I still had it. I found scripture about how the fear of the Lord would help you depart from the snares of death. Another scripture was about people who put darkness for light. Another was about straight is the gate and narrow is the way. Think God was trying to tell me something? I know he was. Think I took heed. No!

I had stopped drinking. Yep, I hadn't had a drink in months. It'd been months since I'd broken up with my friend from above (you remember the one I couldn't have married anyway.) I wasn't real close to God, but I was trying. I'd been praying a little and reading the Bible some. I even wanted to go back to church. I was real depressed about my first husband. He had a baby with this girl he dated. He even married her. I wanted that life! That should have been me! I still loved him. I couldn't stand it. I had to get out. I should have turned to God for comfort, but again I sought comfort with the world. Notice a really bad pattern. I arranged a night out with some girls I worked with. Nope, not the best friend I trusted (she got married). These were people I was acquainted with. They were fun girls and they could get me into any club. We went to some hole in the wall. Why I am not sure. I was even more miserable there than at home. I didn't drink that night, but I got out on the dance floor. These 2 guys followed us back to our table. One of the guys liked me. I really wasn't interested! One of the girls liked his friend. I wasn't interested in either one of them. The only way my friend could get a date with the one guy was if I'd agree to go on a double date with her and the other guy. So I agreed. BIG MISTAKE! A few days later I went to her house and we went to meet these guys at a local restaurant. They were drinking, but I was not. I told them "I stopped drinking months ago!" I really didn't want to drink. They drank beer for about an hour, and then a special waitress came out with a Margarita and gave it to me. I told them I didn't want it. They were saying "come on just one sip, Drink it!" The friend must have told them that was my favorite drink. One sip couldn't hurt, right? Wrong, I don't remember much after that sip. What I do remember is waking up late the next evening in my house with that guy's shirt on! I took me a long time to get myself back together. I called the girl and asked her what happened. She said nothing! She said I drank too much and they drove me home. I knew my limits on alcohol. I didn't even remember anything after the first drink! I could drink three of those and just be tipsy. Something was wrong! She offered to take me to dinner the next night. I in my dazed state of mind agreed. I said do you think I should go to the hospital. She said I was being stupid. She said nothing happened. I knew something was wrong, but I just said "oh well". I never turned to God! About 6 weeks later I was dizzy and tired a lot. She suggested I take a pregnancy test. I promptly told her that was impossible. She said "nothings impossible". I said "I haven't been with anyone in months it is impossible." She said "you need a test". I knew she'd been lying about the night we went out with those guys. I couldn't believe it! We bought a test and sure enough the result was positive. I wanted to die! She came and put her arm around me. I'll never forget what she said "don't worry, I'm off on Thursday I'll take you to get an abortion and nobody has to know!" I became angry so fast! I said, "Are you crazy? I would never kill a baby!" She said "You can't have that baby!" I left in a rage. I wasn't living for God, but I knew abortion was wrong. No, I couldn't even fathom the thought of an abortion. I told my parents, (not about the rape, just the baby) I told my close friends, and I hid from everyone else. I set up a nursery. I was so upset with what he did to me but it was not the baby's fault. I was going to accept it and love it. I know now that he used a date rape drug on me. I found out because I confronted him by phone. I didn't tell him I was pregnant but I lied and told him I had aids. He said coldly "it's nearly impossible for the male to catch that from a woman, I asked my doctor" He also said "You can't prove anything. There's nothing to say it wasn't consensual." I assumed it was too late to get tested for the drug in my system. I never pursued the issue with him. I also never told him I was pregnant. Three months into the pregnancy my ultrasound showed there was a problem. I was so scared. I didn't want anything to be wrong with my baby. I remember my great grandmother saying "Don't worry, I've prayed about it and no baby is there" I ignored her. "She said again, the Lord has showed me there's not a baby there." What did she know? I had several test and finally I learned of my condition. My womb was growing, but the baby wasn't there. The nurse said it's where the body spontaneously aborts the pregnancy! She said it's a common condition. She also said that this can happen when drugs are involved. My blood work was clean and she knew I didn't use drugs. She asked me if I'd experienced a date rape drug. I told her no. My Granny was right! God answered her prayer. My FAITH was tested on abortion. I wasn't living for God; I straddled the fence on lots of issues, but not that one. The good Lord knew that baby wasn't what I needed and he took it from me. If a child's not meant to be in this world the Lord will not let it be born. Having an abortion is like playing "God". We don't have that right! If you think abortion is the answer it's not! Prayer is the answer. I should have taken this lesson from God and repented. I did not. Again, I sought comfort in the world.

I had a career. I loved to work! I knew what I wanted and I knew what it would take to get it! MONEY! I was tired of being poor. I almost had my credit cleaned up from the divorce and was on my way! I had my priorities in order. Too bad they were in the wrong order. I only went to clubs on occasion because every time I went something bad would happen to me. I accepted the fact that going to clubs and drinking was wrong. I knew God wasn't pleased with that. I learned my lesson on those things. You learned earlier I don't go home with men from bars, but the devil does know our weakness. My ex-husband became a big part of my life again. He got divorced from the other girl he was married to. I'd like to say he divorced her before we became close, but that's not true. No, we weren't going to get re-married and I would have been ok if he had worked things out with her. We were now modern open minded folks. We didn't want a relationship with each other. He needed to have some fun and I needed my career. We spent lots of time together when it was convenient. We were happy with what we had. I justified it because we used to be married, he was my husband and he was my first. (There's that justification again.)

God started dealing with me yet again. I tell you this time I wished he would have left me alone. I was happy with the life I found in the world. I had money, I had the freedom to come and go as I chose, lots of fun with my friends, and I still had my first love when I needed him. He was now my best friend. My worldly life was perfect. I had everything a single sinner could want. I tried to ignore that voice from God bidding me back.

God began to deal with me even stronger. It just kept getting more intense. The "x" and I began to have problems and I didn't see him for about 1 month. The Lord was dealing with me so strong I really didn't notice. I kept finding the scripture about straight is the gate and narrow is the way. I started going to church. I even began to wonder if I was lost. I went to the alter one morning and said I repented. I thought that was my salvation. I don't believe you can loose your salvation, but I wondered briefly if I'd ever gotten it to begin with. The very next week my FAITH was tested. I knew I couldn't keep the job I had and live for God. I resigned my position. My last day was on a Friday. That afternoon I was tempted, my last day and I was tempted. I gave into the temptation. Now - I loved my "x" and money more than my God. What was I thinking? I had the fear of God, I knew better. I intentionally sinned against God's warning.

The night I resigned (after giving into temptation) I went to a car show in Gatlinburg with a friend. I knew I would be punished for what I had done. I told her I had to be real careful. Everything went well. I went back the next night. A different friend went with me. We ran into a couple of other friends. A guy she liked and Vance (my husband). On the way home that night I stopped at a shopping center. See Vance had left his vehicle there. He got into it and he went to his home. My friend wanted to ride with the other guy and come to hang out at my house. I said that was fine. They stopped at a store before coming toward my home. I was traveling down a main road in the city. Out of no-where 3 (weighing over 1,000 pounds each) horses hit my car. One smashed in the front of my compact car, one the back and the last once attempted to jump over my car ripping the metal back on impact. It killed all three horses. The horse that ripped the metal off the top of my car landed ½ ways in my car. My scalp was ripped open from the metal. The fesses from the horse ended up getting into my blood. Life as I knew it was over. I was in and out of the hospital for months. I almost died from Ecoli caused by the horse's fesses. I lost my ability to pursue my career, I lost my home, I lost my money, I lost my dignity, and worst of all I lost ability to think and reason. I was unstable mentally. I thought I was so strong within myself, but not without my mental function. I was so scared. The "x" tried to be my friend. But a convenient schedule doesn't work well when you loose your mental control. Every minute felt like hours. There's not much about the next 6 months I remember, but I know some of the facts. One evening some of my friends (the guys from the pool hall mentioned early in my story) brought a guy with them. Someone I'd never met before. Within a week's time from me being released from the hospital the last time I was supposedly married to this guy. I began to regain some of my mental function, as I did a judge quickly annulled the marriage. I was not legally competent enough to be married! What really happened is a pretend marriage gave a predator the keys to my house and access to my bank accounts. I thank God for allowing me to heal enough to get an annulment. I sent a letter to the person that did that forgiving him, sometimes I still can't believe it really happened. I moved into my moms to complete my recovery. I no longer had my career, I had no money, no home, no friends (they turned their backs on me because of the annulment, I don't think they realized how sick I was, they knew this guy. I have to believe they just didn't understand what was going on), I had nothing! I know lots of people were praying for me, but I still refused to give my heart back to God. Even though I didn't turn everything over to God he allowed me to begin healing.

After a couple months at my mom's I was doing much better. I started hanging out with Vance. We went out as friends and ended up married. I believe God sent him to me. Not because I deserved it but because God is FAITHful. I became pregnant with our son. I recovered 100%! I became healthier than I've ever been. I am still very healthy. I should have been praising God! I did not. Even after that it took me awhile to find my way back to God's house.

Vance and I eventually found a little church. The church we currently attend. The church were I had gotten saved several years before. God brought me back to the day and time I got saved. My salvation was real and I never lost it. We went for a few months and were back out again. I knew better. I just didn't give in to the spirit of God. Our marriage needed God. Our life was falling apart. We pretty much hated one another. Vance doesn't believe in divorce. His first divorce was not his choosing. He wasn't going to just leave me. I wanted him to leave. We were miserable! The "x" who had remained my friend through all these years became an issue. We had stayed in touch secretly on occasion. I knew Vance wouldn't approve, but I felt I needed my friend. I should have turned to God, but I didn't. I turned to the "x". I was a lot closer to him than I was to Vance or God. I knew it was wrong.

My marriage seemed to be over. I was thinking seriously about leaving Vance. I thought maybe I was wrong for marrying Vance. He wasn't my first love. That tug on my heart from God just wouldn't go away. I said ok "I'll go to that little church one more time" (I praise God for that little church) I was looking for an answer from God. God sent that answer. The man who preached was a friend. He was my friend, Vance's friend, and even the "x's" friend. That message would not have meant the same coming from anyone else. His message was about being FAITHful to your first love and how your first love should be "GOD". WOW! The message God gave him that night changed my life.

I repented. I had to confess my sin to God and my husband. God worked out my marriage. I was even blessed by seeing Vance get saved. We are happy and our marriage is strong. The Lord has really blessed our family. I still fail God. I sin daily, but I've learned a lot. I try my best to live for God. I want to walk as close to God as I can. I praise God for everything! It's amazing how much patients he has with me. I thank him especially for sending me to a church that is helping me to grow as a Christian. It's a church with old fashioned Christian leadership and the freedom to let the Spirit control the services.

I have learned that when you don't let go of the world you are the one who suffers. You cannot enjoy your salvation neither can you enjoy your worldly life. I wasted several years in that miserable condition. I should have just let God have it. When you get saved and give your heart and soul to God you are his. He will not let go! You must let go of the world or he will make you humble. If you still don't listen the wages for sin is death.

God gave me repeated opportunities. I am not worthy to write a "Christian book", I wasn't worthy of salvation either. It's by Grace through FAITH we are saved. Grace is an undeserved gift. The only begotten son of God died on the cross so we could be saved. None of us deserve God's grace. God loves us enough to give us his grace. I thank God that he loves me! I am also thankful for the blessing and gift of this book. Not because I was allowed to do the typing, but because it is a work God chose me for. I am no more special than you, I don't have your talents, I can't even sing, but God loves all of our souls exactly the same. We are saved into a good work. There is work for all of us to do.

Grace At Eight
Smallwood, Grace – VA

I had attended church every Sunday regularly and enjoyed going. It was just what we did. During a revival at the age of eight (8) I went to the alter and I ask Jesus to forgive me of my sins, come into my heart, and be my Saviour. He did! I am sure he did. My Sunday school teacher wasn't sure, some of our neighbors wasn't sure, but I was sure. They all said I was too young and did not realize what sin was about. I knew that Jesus was my Saviour. I was saved by God's grace! I was baptized in a creek in January. I was always easy to catch a cold, but I did not get sick at all. There were small slivers of ice in the water. The water was so cold, but there was a warmth inside I could not explain. I had a small red backed new testament it was given to me at Sunday school. I'd lay across my bead and read it. There was a peace that was so real. In my teen years I got cold on the Lord and then I pray to try to get close. I realize now there was a war going on . My flesh against my spirit.

I married at the age of fifteen (15). I didn't go back to church for twelve (12) years. I tried to pray from time to time but Heaven seemed to brass. I grew hard. I used bad language and let heart fill with hate. In short I was a far cry from that eight (8) year old little girl. Now peace was totally absent from my life. Everything was a mess.

I began to have a dream. I dreamed Jesus was coming back for his church. I don't know how often I had these dreams. Jesus was closer and closer. When I dreamed it the first time he was just a small speck in the sky. As I dreamed this more frequent he became closer and I got to the point that I could awake myself. I'd tell myself to wake up, It's that dream again! The last time I had the dream it was not a dream but a vision. I awoke myself as I had many times before. I sat up in bed to the left side of the room I saw the door that let outside to the pasture, to the right side of the room I could see the furniture and the doorway that led to the kitchen. The rest of the house straight in front of me was like a real foggy day. In that fog was a great cloud of Jesus and his angels around him. "Oh my God I've waited too late!" I heard myself say. I reached to touch him and it all vanished. I got up went inside the laundry room which was on the side of the room where the vision was. I fell on my face in the pile of dirty laundry I asked for Jesus to please forgive me and take me back. All I could understand was a verse of scripture from the Bible that said something about "doing your first works over" I said o.k. Lord I'll go to church and if you speak to my heart during alter call I'll go to the alter and depend on you to do the rest. I did and he did. As soon as I knelt at the alter a deacon came to talk to me. I raised my head long enough to say "sir, I mean you no disrespect but I did not come here t talk to you but Jesus" I don't know how long I prayed but when I got up I know Jesus had forgiven me. I was baptized again. A while after that I promised Jesus that with his help I'd do my best to live for him the rest of my life. That is a promise I mean to keep as long as I live in this life. I want a closer walk with Jesus every day of my life because Jesus is my life now and always. {**Author's Note**: This is my grand-mother. A remarkable woman.}

The Secret Prayer
Tolliver, Gary - TN

Hi. My name is Gary. I was saved when I was twelve (12) years old at a revival at Clear Branch Baptist Church. They were having a revival and I had been under conviction for a while. I was asking my mother questions. My mom would go up to the barn every evening to milk the cow and pray. I thought she had a boyfriend or someone she was talking to all the time. Boy did she it was "God"! I sneaked up there one day to peep and see who it was. As I crawled in under some loose boards on the barn I could see her. She was down on her knees, (not caring about the cow manure) crying out to God on my behalf. She said "God my son Gary is asking questions." I got so scared I ran out of that barn not caring or thinking about if she heard me. On a Wednesday night in May 1965 I ran to the alter. I tell people I got saved at a high rate of speed because God saved me running down the aisle. He has been with me ever since. I have left him, but he has never left me. Salvation is the most important thing in our lives. God Bless! {**Author's Note**: Praise God for his good old fashioned praying Mama)

Follow Your Heart
Tolliver, Phyllis - TN

My name is Phyllis. I was saved about forty-five (45) years ago. I was eight (8) years old in a school revival at Maynardville Baptist. I went to church that day and heard the gospel. I got under conviction and was literally scared to death. I was afraid of what my friends and other people would say so I did not go to the alter that day. That night I went to bed early because I shared a bed with my two (2) sisters. I crawled under the cover and cried out to God for mercy. I told God If I felt the same drawing power tomorrow I promised God I would go to the alter. The next service God was drawing me. I did get up and go to the alter but not without a fight from the devil. I said "I don't care what you say I'm going so I got up and went." I was so happy! I went home to tell my mom and dad who where in a back-slidden condition. Mom said you don't know what you are talking about. You are too young! She was wrong. You see my mom planted a seed of doubt without knowing it. That seed came back to haunt me. When I got twelve (12) (for some reason people in my generation thought you had to be twelve (12) maybe because Christ was in the temple teaching when he was twelve (12), who knows.) I went to the alter at Union Baptist to try to get saved. God said "you are saved!" I got up and this went on for about ten (10) years. My son was born. The devil throwed that seed in my face again. I prayed for three (3) months "Please Lord, if I am not saved save me and if I am give me something or do something so I will know without any doubt." I started to a revival at Blaine Chapel Missionary Baptist Church. I believe Fate Oaks held the revival or was the pastor. I don't know, but praise be to God on the way down Tazewell Pike I prayed "Please Lord let this be the night." The first song they sang I felt the Holy Ghost from my head to my toes. When I came back to this earth I was hugging some older lady. They told me I shouted all over the church. I don't remember that but I can still see this lady in my memory bank. The devil has never ever been able to make me doubt I got saved, not since that glorious night. You see

I knew God answered my prayers. I had felt his presence before but not in this powerful way. I hope we can learn two (2) lessons from reading this. 1.) Be careful what we say and do to a child 2.) Ask if we want something from God. God has no respect of persons. He is my closest and dearest friend. With Love, Phyllis. {**Author's Note**: Our children are our most precious gift. My thought on this would be keep them in church, have FAITH, do your best to raise them right, and they will work out their own salvation with God.}

I Love the Lord
Wallace, Rozella –TN

I was saved when I was young. The Lord put me under conviction in my younger years. At first I ran from God. One night I went to church with my dad and mom. The preacher was giving an alter call. I was about 11 or 12 years old. I was so scared. I was shaking, but I couldn't stand still. I ran to the alter and gave my heart to God and when I raised up I had a feeling in my heart like never before. Everything looked so different to me. I had a happy feeling about me after that. I loved the Lord and did my best to live for him.

As I grew older I drifted away from him and went out into the world. I lived for the devil for many years. Then when I was in my early thirties I met my husband. We both made it right with God. We got married and we have tried our best to live as close to God as we could. God has helped us so much in our lives. We had blessing miracles and heartaches, but he has always been there for us. Without the Lord I just couldn't make it on my own. I've failed him many times, but he has always taken me back and forgave me. Today I can say I am a child of God and I intend to stay that way 'cause this old world can't last much longer. I want to live the rest of my life for "God." Amen! {**Author's Note**: I haven't known Ms. Wallace long, but it only takes one time to know that the spirit of God lives within her heart. She is a blessing to be around.}

The Quarter
Tharp, Doris – TN

I have trouble remembering my childhood. I do remember vaguely mom and dad taking our family of eight (8) to church. I have no medical reason that keeps me from remembering things. I just don't remember. One memory that has stuck with me is one I would like to share with you.

As a small child around nine (9) years old the family left Union County to a home in Knoxville. Immediately I became friends to the family next door. Especially a lady named June McClain. I remember the family was not going to church at the time but, June invited me to go with her. I started gong to church with her at a little Baptist church up the road. I remember that she and I went for a while. Then one Sunday my family visited the little church. I remember meeting a lot of good people. As a small child I just thought church was somewhere I could go and play with other children. Then one Saturday I remember being in the back yard and Dad had gave me a quarter. I was throwing it in the air and trying to catch it I dropped it and could not find it I remember at church hearing people pray and asking God to help them. I didn't have an understanding of why. I thought that I would just ask God to help me find my quarter. As soon as I asked God for help & opened my eyes and there was my quarter. It was shining as though it was big. I thought no more about asking God to help me that day.

The next day at church I remember I was setting about the fourth (4th) seat back and the right side. We had a visiting preacher that morning. As he preached I tried to whisper and play, but here was some reason I just couldn't this morning. He preached on how God loved us and told how he gave his son so we could be saved. Then he gave an alter call. I remember that I could see the quarter from the day before. I didn't understand at the time what was going on but my heart felt like it was coming out of my chest. It seemed as though I stood there for a long time trying to hold the bench. I finally gave in and went to the alter. I asked Jesus to come in my heart. I was saved at the young age of ten (10). I still think of that shining quarter that was lost. God showed me that I was just as lost as that quarter was and by coming and asking for his help that he would save me. We must be lost before we can be found. When he found me I was shining just as that quarter that was lost. {**Author's Note**: I've attended church with Doris for several years now. Doris is consistent in her work for God and always willing to pitch in and help out.}

Obey the Voice of God
Williams, Jackie – TN

This is my testimony. The Lord saved my soul! I worked at a nursing home. Sister Edna Dyer got onto me about coming to church. I went to get her to quit inviting me. I didn't know what to expect. My brother came to me and asked me if I had been saved. I said no. He took me to the alter and I knelt in prayer. The Lord hadn't dealt with me. I felt alright (I didn't feel bad before I prayed.) I thought I was saved. I went for a year or two thinking I was saved. I went every time the doors was open.

I went to church one night and one of my brothers went to the alter. I went to pray for him. I stepped back out of the way. The Lord spoke to me for the first time. Jesus let me know that I was lost. I said Lord I'll do anything that you want me to do if you'll forgive me. The voice said shake Billy's hand. There was three (3) people named Billy at the service. I knew which one it was. I obeyed and when I did the Lord entered my heart. I was deceived for a couple of years thinking I was saved. A lot of people would say that was a bad thing, but it kept me in church under the preached word until God got ready to deal with me. When God came to me and showed me for sure I was lost I was ready. God told me to shake Billy's hand. That's seems small but no matter how small you should do it if God tells you to do it. It doesn't matter if God says raise your hand, shake somebody's hand, tell somebody you love them my advise is to do it. I got out of church for a long time.

I didn't raise my first (1st) son in church. He's out there lost now, but one day I will hear that he's been saved because the Lord made me that promise. I told you I was out of church for a long time. God brought me back in.

I was at work one night and God told me that if something happened to my family I couldn't pray for them. I was on 3rd shift. I told God if he'd take me off 3rd shift I'd go back to church. That next week I got put on day shift. I went back. I was scared not to. I went back to church for a couple of months and it didn't' feel like God had really accepted me back. I began to pray in bed one night "God I told you I'd go back to church, what do you want from me." I heard a voice say "obey". I thought a minute. I said no that ain't big enough. I prayed the same prayer again. The voice again said "obey". I understood.. I told the Lord I'll go back to church and whatever I feel like doing I'm going to do it. I went to church that night he told me to raise my hand and when I did God forgave me. I've been going ever since. {**Author's Note**: Jackie is one of the deacons at my little church. Jackie is very old fashioned in values and stern in his FAITH. His heart belongs to God and he meant every word mentioned above.}

I Gave My Life To The Lord
Williams, Jon – TN

I have been to church a lot. I went with my brother and his girl-friend then I started going with my parents when I was ten (10) years old. They really went every time the doors was open. Of course I didn't like to go there for a year or two then I actually got into it. Then when I was 15 the church was standing around the alter and the last person I remember talking to me is a girl that I've had a crush on about all my life. She asked me if I needed to be saved and I said yes. They started singing a song and I went and gave my life to the Lord. One last thing I would like to add is get right or get left! Which means get right with God or get left behind. {**Author's Note**: Jon is a good kid. He one of few teenagers that spend his weekends at church with his parents. He is active in the church and is growing as a Christian.}

I Really Got Saved
Williams, Rosella - TN

I went to church all my life. When I was eight (8) years old the Lord dealt with my heart and I thought I got saved! I kept going to church then went to a revival the Lord told me to go the alter and I went. That's when I really got saved. I was seventeen (17) years old. I thank the Lord for that! I don't know what would have happened to me if I didn't. {**Author's Note**: Rosie is one of my best friends. If our church is a well oiled machine – she is the oil. She makes sure everyone stays in touch and keeps our prayer line going.}

The Best Thing
Williford, Carla – TN

I was in the 5th grade when the Lord saved me. That was the best thing that has ever happened to me. There is more I'd like to tell you. 2005 was the worst year of my life. It seemed like the closer I tried to get to God the more the devil was trying to tempt me. I broke my leg on two (2) separate occasions! The Lord gave me the ability to keep going and the strength to keep coming to church. My mamaw went to be with the Lord in August of 2005. It was just by the strength of the Lord I made it through. I guess I am trying to say that the Lord will take care of you no matter what. When things are going bad and you don't think you can go another step keep praying and always have FAITH. God is still doing miracles. My God bless each person and family. {**Author's Note**: Carla teaches Sunday School for the little kids. She works hard to make that class entertaining and spiritually educational for the kids.}

A Criminal Purified
Name Withheld – TN

I am forty-seven (47) years old. I lived most of my life in sin. When I was very young a fire separated me from my family. I was sent to live with my grandmother in West Virginia. I was saved while at her home. I ran away from her house at age thirteen (13). I have lived on my own since then. I have stolen, robbed, and done whatever else it took to survive. I spent ten (10) years in jail. I was released from jail and moved to Tennessee. I began to sale drugs. I enjoyed the life I had I was making about $10,000 every week. Sometimes God would come back to my memory, but I just pushed him away. God got my attention October 22, 2004. God showed me that he and not I was in control. My brother and I had committed a crime and had some extra money. Me, my brother, and my girlfriend went to a local restaurant to have a few drinks and get some food. On the way home (we were driving 55 or 60 mph) she jumped from the car! Yes, she jumped from the car! She was killed! I questioned oh God why? A couple of days after that I was arrested and jailed for failure to pay tickets for possession charges. I was in jail for 49 days. The first 45 I slept. Then a preacher came around talking about

49

Jesus. There in that jail I gave my heart back to Jesus. My life is now so much different. I thank God for all he's done for me. {**Author's Note**: I met this man 2 times. The first time I asked him for his testimony. The next time he was giving his testimony in my little church. He is strong in his FAITH. I believe God is really upon his heart.}

Wait For God
Name Withheld – TN

I met my husband when I was only fourteen (14). I was young, immature, and thought I knew what was best for me. I knew it all! This man was my first, my everything. There was something I was missing. I had an emptiness in my heart. I thought a baby would fill that emptiness in my heart. I became pregnant. I had my first child at the age of fifteen (15). I loved her and she was so precious. Things got complicated. I had to go to school, work, and raise a child. I had very little time for anything else. I did have my mom, Thank God! I knew that she was my baby and I had to be the one who cared for her.

At seventeen (17) I received my General Education Degree and started working full time. I was making very little income. My boyfriend the baby's daddy was still around but he managed to get around (know what I mean.) When I first became pregnant I thought I could talk my mom into signing into letting me and my boyfriend get married. Her reply was "just because you got pregnant doe not me I'm signing you away. I don't believe in having a baby out of wed lock, but I will not allow you to get married." Thank God she didn't. We would have never made it.

We did get married when I turned eighteen (18). By the time I was nineteen (19) we were having our second child. I was living in a home where drugs and alcohol were in use and were being sold by my husband. We fussed and argued constantly. He always wanted to go out with his friends. There was no trust in me for him. I continued to stay and he continued to cheat on me. Yes, we would separate but we always got back together.

I'm not saying he was the only one living wrong. I too would use drugs and drink alcohol occasionally. I did it to fit in and I did it to fill the emptiness I was still feeling from years ago. I would go to church off and on. As soon as I left church I was sinning. My husband was still selling drugs. I knew I wasn't doing nothing about it. The money was great in my eyes!

When I turned twenty-one (21) we had just gotten back to together from a separation. I left him for two (2) months because he had cheated. At first he done everything that I asked of him. I hadn't forgiven him and everyday that passed I was hating him more. I didn't have Christ in my life. I had set him aside once again.

I wasn't going to church and I and been doing drugs and alcohol again. I was ready to give up on our marriage. I spoke to my mom and she convinced me to come back to church and pray about my marriage before walking away. I started going back to church, but I still wasn't being FAITHful to God. I still wasn't putting God first. We know our God is a jealous God. I had finally forgiven my husband and about two (2) months later he went to jail for selling drugs. I thought my world was ending. I had no where to turn but to God. God had a plan for me. During the seven (7) months my husband was gone I found Jesus! Yes, I was baptized at a young age and raised in church, and thought I was saved, but I wasn't! This time I really got saved!

I started going back to church on a regular basis. One week in November they was having a revival. Earlier that week I had been in a car accident. The night I got saved everything was going wrong. Satan did try his hardest that night to keep me away fro the church. I was so determined. I made it to church and I got saved that night! The emptiness that I had been feeling for so long was finally filled. I found Jesus and his love!

I can't say that everything has been easy since that night, but with God I my life it sure has opened a lot of doors for me. My husband came home after spending his seven(7) months. He was a different man. It wasn't the same man I knew before. He had changed for the better. Then he started running with his old friends. He began to go into the places he shouldn't and once again cheated! I was heart-broken. I didn't understand how or why he was cheating. This time he denied it. I already knew, but I tried to forget about it.

I began to pray and ask God to put my mind at ease. My husband was telling me he wasn't cheating, but my heart was telling me something different. Two (2) months went by and then my husband came home and told me he had to tell me something. He said he didn't want to tell me, but God wanted him to. I knew what he was going to say. He told me I was right about him cheating just a few months before. I didn't even cry. I left the room and thanked God for hearing my prayer. I stayed with him once again.

A year went by and I was going to start college. That was made possible by God. Just as it was time for me to enroll I found out that my husband had cheated again. By this time he had done it so many times it didn't surprise me. Yes, it still hurt and I still couldn't understand why. We separated for a couple of months again. God gave me strength I never knew I had.

I was driving home one day and praying. I began to ask God questions. Why my husband cheated? Why couldn't I be enough for him? Before I could get the next question out of my mouth God answered "but how many times have I forgiven you." I didn't know if I could forgive my husband again. I drove and I cried as God was there comforting me.

I remember praying asking God to take any feeling that I had for my husband away. I was tired of hurting. I also prayed for him to save my husband if he wasn't no matter if it meant taking his family. My feeling for my husband began changing that same week. God began to work. I had no desire to be with my husband. I stayed because I was waiting on God to show me my next move.

My husband was back in church and doing everything right. It still didn't change the way I felt. Then finally I knew what God wanted me to do. I told my husband I wasn't happy and I wanted him to leave. He did. I had a feeling of peace that came over me. I knew it was part of God's plan.

A few weeks went by and God convicted me of something I had done in the past. I had sinned against my husband. I had already asked God for forgiveness and thought that was enough, but it wasn't. In this case I had to tell my husband and get his forgiveness. I told him. At first we didn't talk but, I gave him his space and he finally came around. He forgave me. Shortly afterwards we got back together and tried to work things out.

I started getting my feeling back for him. We both could tell we were off to a new start. You see if we will wait upon God and listen for his voice everything will work out to the good. We all have wrong about us, but we must ask God for forgiveness and God will forgive. I believe if I hadn't confessed my sin to my husband that our marriage would have never made it. We are still in church today and our FAITH is growing as our spiritual walk too.

I guess what I'm trying to get across is people always take the easy way out. We have to climb the mountain to reach the top. If we were never in the valley then we would never enjoy the mountain. May God be with you in everything you do. God bless!

CHAPTER 2

PHYSICAL HEALING
THROUGH FAITH

*{James 5:14-15 Is any sick among you? let him call for
the elders of the church; and let them pray over him,
anointing him with oil in the name of the Lord: and the
prayer of FAITH shall save the sick, and the Lord shall
raise him up; and if he have committed sins,
they shall be forgiven him.}*

God Performed a Miracle in My Life
Bernadine, Doris J – VA

The testimony your about to read is not just a testimony it is
a divine supernatural miracle from God. I've read stories in
magazines of others shared the events of their FAITH and courage.
The very word miracle catches our eyes to print. Miracles are meant
to be shared. When a miracle happens in our lives our FAITH seems
to explode.

The eighteenth (18th) day of June, 1984 will forever be embedded
into my memory. That is the day God performed a miracle in my
life. I had been under a doctor's care for headaches for seven years.

Every time I would go for a visit he increase the pain medication. I only grew worse. Then on June 18, 1984 I awakened with the most indescribable pain in my head. I have never known pain like that before. I managed to get out of bed and called to my teenage daughter to call an ambulance. I told her to call my husband who was at work. I then fell unconscious to the floor. I learned later the ambulance came and took me to the hospital. With extensive CAT scan they found blood in the brain and the spinal column. I learned they let me lay for seven days trying to get me to stabilize. Then they did a test and it was discovered I had an aneurysm above my right eye. My family was told that it was inoperable. They were told to call my immediate family who lived in Virginia. I lived in Michigan at the time. The neurosurgeon told my husband and children if they did operate I could die on the table or be confined to a wheelchair for life. Thanks be unto God he was in control. I am so glad my relationship with him was one of trust. I knew I was his child. I became a Christian at the age of 19. I was now 46. I had taught Sunday school, and played the organ at my church. Many people were praying for me. The neurosurgeon told my family of a method they used in the 1950's. They would go in the neck and clamp off the artery that was feeding the aneurysm and that there would be three crucial days of waiting. The clamp would need to be turned once a day, and after 3 days if it did not take hold there was nothing else they could do. My church, loved ones, and friends continued to intercede for me and God granted their prayers. I truly believe an angel of the Lord turned that clamp each day. The doctors were amazed I spent 21 days in the hospital many of those in intensive care, lost 23 pounds, but God be the Glory. I left the hospital with no side effects! **I was totally healed!** The only reminder is a three inch scar on my neck. It's as small as a hairline it looks like a crease on my skin. I was able to return to church and rejoice with everyone who had prayed for my healing. I've always known he was a God of miracles. I'm so glad he loved me enough to let me witness his miraculous touch. He is the giver of life. My life will never be the same. I have never ceased to tell others. He still gives miracles today. If you believe and expect it then it will surely happen. I know! I am his witness! My prayer is as you read my testimony may God quicken your FAITH to receive your healing, your answered prayer, or his miracle for you. The most wonderful thing about my healing is every time I tell it or put it in print I get healed all over again. I give him thanks! {**Author's Note**: I've never met this woman, but her testimony made me praise God!}

He is the God of All Comfort
Blanton, Ida –VA

Many times in my life I have had to depend on the Lord for more than a few of my needs. My daughter had gotten a bad doctor's report. I understood that it was cancer. It was on my mind the first thing when I awoke in the mornings and the last thing on my mind when went to sleep. One Sunday morning I felt that I couldn't carry the load any longer. I was watching a program and the preacher gave an invitation to pray. I got down on my knees in my living room. I told God I could not handle it any longer. I told him that I needed to give my burden to him. God told me that Lorene would be alright. A peace come over me and I didn't worry about it anymore. God didn't speak out loud but by the peace that came over me was him and by his spirit he spoke to me. The words that came to me were Lorene is going to be alright. If we give our worries to Jesus he will take care of them. {**Author's Note**: I don't know much about Ida, but I do know that she is a prayer warrior.}

30 Minutes Away
Fletcher, Floyd – TN

My miracle happened on Tazewell pike in Knoxville, Tennessee. My mother was dying. The doctors said she was having a heart attack, internal bleeding, and a high fever.

I prayed to the Lord. I knew about many times in the Bible God healed the sick. I knew all God had to do was speak the words and my mother would be healed. I asked the Lord to heal my mother as he had done for others in the Bible. The God we serve has no respect of persons.

I was about thirty (30) minutes from the hospital when I began praying this prayer to the Lord. I finally got there and my mother said "I'm having the best day I've had since I've been here." I said

"when did you start feeling better?" She said "about thirty (30) minutes ago." The doctor came in and said she is not having a heart attack, and we find no internal bleeding, and her fever is gone. She went home two (2) days later. Thank You Lord! {**Author's Note**: The key here is that Floyd has the FAITH. FAITH is the key to everything!}

His Mighty Power
Fultz, Ella –VA

Thank God for his mighty power! There are so many wonderful things he has done in my life. He healed me when I was a three and one/half year (3.5) year old girl. We were walking to my grandmother's house one day and everything was fine. It was a beautiful day. My mom and siblings were by my side. The whole world was an adventure to me. Life for me was about to change. My legs began to grow tired and my whole body began to hurt. Mom thought I was tired from too much fun. Things went from bad to worse. They took me to the hospital. The doctors told my parents the bad news. I had Polio! Polio is a crippling disease. It would leave me with at best weak limbs and maybe in a wheel chair the rest of my life. I was in a hospital in Lexington, Kentucky. This was a few hundred miles from where we lived.

This was taking place in the 1950's. Times were very hard. My dad couldn't afford to buy a car. If they went very far they paid someone else to take them. One day after I had been in the hospital for a while mom and dad got the call. Come get your daughter she is wearing braces and doing fine. My dad and mom were Bible believing prayer warriors! Dad had said all along she will not come home wearing braces or in a wheel chair. He believed in Divine healing.

When they got to the hospital dad waited in a little room while mom went with the nurse to get me. Other people were waiting in the room where dad was and every time they heard the sound of someone walking down the hall with the sound of clicking (you know braces) they would say here she comes. Dad would say, No, that not her she is healed. Meanwhile back in the place where I was I had my braces on and ready to go. The nurse said ok, let's go.

When she put me down from off the table where I was sitting my feet touched the floor and I fell down. I could not walk with those braces on. The nurse said I don't know what to do. The doctor has gone and won't be back today. At that very moment out of my 3 year old mouth I said, let me down I can walk! She said honey; you can't even walk with your braces on. I said let me down I can walk! So just to please me she put me back down. **I took off walking as if I had never had Polio!** There was not a dry eye in the room. There were tears of joy and thankfulness. God had healed me completely. There's not a trace, not even at limp. Nothing would indicate that I have ever had polio. The same God that healed me can heal you! If you need a miracle by FAITH in God and his word nothing is impossible for God! Who couldn't love a God like that? May God richly bless you! Prayerfully yours, Ella Fultz. {**Author's Note**: Wow! That's all I can say just Wow!}

The Heart Attack
Graves, Carolyn –TN

On July 31, 2005 I had a massive heart attack. I went to the hospital the doctor did a test and found I was still having the attack. The main artery was 100% blocked. I had two more that was 85% and another that was 75% blocked. The doctor's told my children they would treat them with medication. I was there for a week. I came home on Friday and I awoke on Saturday morning with chest pain. I went to the emergency room had another test the next day. The doctor found an artery blocked 100% at the back of my heart. He could not open this one the only way was surgery. My blood was too thin to have surgery. I could bleed to death My chest pain started again he had to do the surgery any way. He told my family there was not much hope.

Everyone started praying. My family, my church, my friends and my pastor (God bless him) were praying. The doctor came out and told my family I had a massive heart attack. He said a woman hardly ever makes it. My pastor came back and prayed for me. I knew I was going to be o.k. before they went into surgery. They let my family come back. The waiting room was full. The doctor commented on my big family. My sister Margie from Indiana came up to my bed and prayed for me. When she finished she said Carol you are going to be ok. God has not brought you his far to let you go now. Don't remember her praying, I don't remember the family even being there.

When I came out of surgery the only thing I remember is my pastor praying and saying the words "God didn't bring you this far to let you go now." God wanted me to remember this. The doctor's did all they could and God did the rest. God is with you in everything you go through. If you will just let him be. Prayer changes things. Thanks to everyone for your prayers. {**Author's Note**: I visited Carolyn while this was going on. She never seemed scared. That takes true FAITH. I just wonder if mine would have been that strong in her situation. Would yours?}

The Car Ran Over Me.
Graves, Carolyn –TN
I was twenty one (21) years old and while crossing the street I was hit by a car. I was dragged under the car for one-hundred (100) feet. About every bone in my body was broken. I had head injuries. I was in the emergency room all day. They were trying to repair me. The doctor came out and told my husband they had done all they could do. He said God as going to have to take over. God did just that. God has never let us down. I was kept asleep for about two (2) weeks when they let me wake up. I was a mess broken bones everywhere. My head busted, my ears was damaged. I couldn't hear from one ear at all. My husband had never left the hospital at all. Everyone told me he was sick the whole time. Later came the best part and made everything worth it all. My husband got saved in my hospital room in the bathroom. I was getting better everyday. This was one among many more miracles God has performed in my life. {**Author's Note**: I am sure this is one of the things that makes her FAITH as strong as it is. God certainly has her here for a reason.}

The Prayer Line
Hensley, Lannie –TN
I thank my Lord Jesus Christ for my Christian life and for each day he lets me live. I think we take that for granted. The Lord has

been there so many times for me and my family. I don't know what I would do without him. The week of Christmas 2005 I went in for a stress test. When I got home that evening the heart doctor's nurse called she said the doctor wanted to see me. I knew something was wrong. I just fell apart. The human side took over and my FAITH got weak. My husband and I went to his office. The doctor said the test showed the artery in front of my heart was blocked and he would know more what he would have to do after additional testing.

My husband called my sisters and they got a prayer line going for me. I thank God for everyone who prayed for me. You see God heard the prayers! I felt a change in my body the day before the additional testing. I was so upset I didn't fully realize what had happened. I went to the hospital still crying and praying. They took me back and the doctor started the additional testing but didn't see any blockage. Again, he looked and said "I don't see any blockage!" The doctor seemed amazed. I cried out loud "Thank you God!" I'm so glad when my FAITH was weak I had God's people praying for me. {**Author's Note**: I've known Lannie for years. She is most definitely one who believes in prayer and knows God's still performing miracles.}

The Power Of Prayer
Hodge, Jack – TN

Johnathan Bond has a testimony that is guaranteed to keep a crowds attention. Morning Star recording artist Johnathan Bond of Young Harmony, CCMA Duo of the year, has a story for you. On September 24, 1991, while driving on rain slick roads, an 18-wheeler pulled into Johnathan's lane on a four lane highway and forced him into oncoming traffic. His car was hit by two different vehicles with a force so great that is ripped his seat belt in half. The next thing Johnathan remembers, "was lying on a wet road and people were standing over him trying to find a pulse." After a few minutes of CPR, the paramedics said, "We can't do anything for him, he's dead." At that moment Johnathan heard a voice speak to him that said repeatedly, "ask and you shall receive." Remembering the teachings of the Word, Johnathan pleaded, "Lord, if You will save me and let me live, I'll live for You." When his mother arrived at the emergency room and asked about her son, the doctor put his arm around her and assured her that the ER team had done all they could but they had lost him. Johnathan's mother heard the same voice speak to her, The same words, "ask and you shall receive". She then asked the doctor, who was a Christian, to pray with her for her son. Although he was simply being nice, as they prayed, a nurse ran up to the doctor and exclaimed, "That man is not dead!" Johnathan had began to strangle while the nurse was preparing his body for identification. PRAISE GOD! Johnathan was then placed in the Intensive Care Unit. After further examination the doctor told Mrs. Bond, "Although God has answered our prayers and brought back your son, he would probably be better off dead". Johnathan's injuries were extensive and massive. He had a brain aneurysm from a fractured skull. His head was swollen past his shoulders. His right eye was loosed from the socket and was being held with two out of 50 ligaments. His face was cut, two ribs, his right arm and shoulder had been broken. His back was broken in nine places and he was paralyzed from right above his waist down. The most critical was oxygen had been cut off to his brain for approximately 18 minutes. The doctor said, "Ms. Bond, there is no way." Three days after the accident, while in Intensive Care, Johnathan's heart stopped and the doctors rushed in to try to revive him. Without success. The doctor informed his mom once again that they had lost him. She said, "Do you remember the first day I came in here? Will you pray with me again?" The doctor, Johnathan's mom and a non-christian nurse began to pray. As they prayed GOD brought Johnathan back once again. Four days after his wreck, Johnathan walked out of the hospital. Completely healed from head to toe. No surgeries by man, just the GREAT PHYSICIAN, JESUS! GOD IS SO AWESOME!

God has His ways of getting our attention when He has a job for us. Sometimes we don't listen and He uses great measures to wake us up. Is God speaking to you? What does He have in store for you? Is there a job He wants you to do? Listen. Accept the calling. Your rewards are beyond your wildest dreams.

I've been a friend of Johnathan and Ginger for 4 years. As far as I'm Concern, you could not ask for a more devoted couple to Gods work. Johnathan is a man of his word. Johnathan and his beautiful wife Ginger live for the Lord and spreads the word through song and testimony. You could not ask for a more humble man than Johnathan {**Author's Note**: I think this has been said before, but nothing is too hard for God!}

There's a Reason
Hodge, Linda – TN (Written by Jack Hodge)

In April,2005 Linda had a routine mammogram and was told it was suspicious but the radiologist was not sure and they were sending the test to New York for a further reading. Two weeks later New York returned their opinion that Linda probably had breast cancer and needed a biopsy.

A biopsy was done and she did have cancer. However, the type of cancer Linda had was extremely rare. She did not have a lump as most breast cancers are, she had little freckle like spots in her breast. The surgeon scheduled a lumpectomy and afterwards Linda was referred to an Oncologist and was told that the Doctor recommended she have both breast removed because even though the cancer was only in one breast it would develop in the other breast as well. She was also told that she could elect to take a medication for 5 years instead and the doctor gave Linda a week to decide what she wanted to do. Well, any woman in this situation would say write me the prescription! When Linda went back with her decision the Doctor told her he would not recommend this choice because the type of cancer she had would not show up on a mammogram. This puzzled Linda as her cancer was first diagnosed through a routine mammogram! Linda went to another Oncologist for a second opinion. This doctor told Linda that the type of cancer she had would not respond to radiation but that enough was not known about this type of cancer to say if it would spread to the other breast or not. Linda was given a prescription for Tamoxifen that day.

In July Linda was sent to have an MRI done on her breast and the results came back that all of the cancer cells had not been removed and she still had cancer in the same breast. Linda was sent for additional more compressed mammogram and Ultra Sound. The morning before she was to report to the hospital to have these test done Linda was in the shower and she lifted her hands to God and prayed as she cried for him to wash her body clean of its impurities and to make her whole again. She dropped her arms and it was just like the Spirit said Get those arms back up! She lifted her arms again and continued praying until she felt the Spirit was ready for her to stop.

The next day when she went to the hospital for her tests there was a young lady named Betty who walked into the mammogram room. This was special to her as Betty had been with her throughout this whole ordeal. Betty did two views and said she would be back as she was taking them to Dr. Norris (whom is a radiologist which had come in from Knoxville just to read Linda's results) to view. Linda asked Betty if her husband Jack could come in and wait with her and was told sure and Jack was brought into the room. Betty came back in shortly and said that Dr. Norris decided he needs more views but this time with more magnification. This means they needed more compression. Linda's breast were extremely sore from all the testing and from the surgery. When Betty started Linda started to cry and Betty asked Jack to hold her. When Linda looked at Betty she was crying also. She told Jack that she knew how Linda felt as she had to go through this herself once. Betty told Jack that it felt like someone was stabbing Linda with a knife in the breast and Linda said she was exactly right. Anyway, she finished the views and again took them to Dr. Norris to view. When Betty came back in she said Dr. Norris now wanted to do the Ultrasound. The technician who did the Ultrasound could not find anything so she called Dr. Norris in and he did the ultrasound himself. After about 5 minutes he said I cant find anything. He said the MRI must have given us a false positive on the 5mm spot. Linda looked at Jack and they both smiled because they knew where the spot went. It went down the drain in the shower the night before as Linda lifted her arms to God. Dr. Norris told her to go home and not to worry that Linda was leaving the hospital with good news. Dr. Norris told Linda he was not going to do a biopsy because he could not find anything to biopsy. Linda's Oncologist called her later that day and said they would do another MRI in 6 months. The additional testing was done in six months and Linda still remains cancer free. Not only is she cancer free but her breast has completely filled in and reshaped and, get this, the scar is disappearing as well.

Linda knows that God has a reason for everything that happens to us. She feels that the reason will be revealed someday. Until then, she tells everyone about what her precious Saviour has done for her and who knows, maybe this is why it happened; so Linda could just gives her testimony to others and praises God for his mercy and love.

God Is God
Mashburn, April Houser – TN

My name is April. I was saved when I was nine years old in a little church back in Knoxville. I remember it well, it was during a Vacation Bible School, at Independent Calvary Baptist Church and John Bright was our pastor. I have a testimony that I do hope and pray that touches someone's heart.

I was involved in a car accident many years ago that changed my life. I was a happy go lucky seventeen-year-old girl that had graduated from high school in May not knowing that the next year my life would change forever. While dating my fiancé, I worked at a local deli, where he was a bag boy. I would wake up in the morning at my house would usually tell my parents whatever I could to get them not to ask questions and then I was gone for the entire day. Usually, we would stay for a while at my future husbands house and then go to some of our friend's homes. We were always together that is, if we could be.

Although, I never had time for church, I was always too involved with my social life for taking time to go to church. I would always pray for my food before I ate and pray each night before I slept and morning before I started my day but that was the extent of it all.

One day after my fiancé and I left work we drove up to his house up in Luttrell. We were at his house for a little while when we decided to leave anyway he wanted me to drive back. I do not recollect exactly where we were going from there but he did not want to drive he had been to the doctor the day before and he did not feel well, so, I agreed with him and we were off. As, we approached the intersection of Walker Ford Road and Maynardville Hwy. I was stopped at the stop sign and a white car came traveling east with their turning signal on. Well, I pulled out and they did not turn. We were hit, my side of the car was smashed in and it was not believable that I was alive. My fiancé died instantly, at least that is what I was told. I was told that LifeStar came and picked me up and I woke up five days later at the University of Tennessee Hospital.

When I woke up I did not know what was going on. I did not know where I was. The only thing I knew was that my Mother and my Father was right there by my side with me, just like they had always tried to be. I was moved to Fort Sanders Hospital to their unit called Patricia Neal Rehabilitation Unit. There I would undergo weeks of therapy. I remember very plainly being told of the many prayers that were told on my part. I thank all who prayed for me. I thought I was younger than I actually was, I really thought I was six years younger than that of my age of seventeen. I had put it all out of my mind. I received a closed head injury. My parents were told that I would never recover. But, by the GRACE of GOD I did!

There was a therapist there and I remember her name to this day, Renee Seeke, she made me keep on going to my therapy appointments when I wanted to stop. I went from a wheelchair to a walker to a cane in a few weeks. I also had a board with all the letters of the alphabet on it so I could point at letters to be able to speak to people. I would not be able to do this if it was not for all the prayers that were prayed for me. I asked many questions as to why I was at the hospital and what had happened. I did not completely remember everything that had happened. My Mother and Father took many pictures of my family and friends, looking at them now I am slightly embarrassed by the way I looked at the time. My parents would allow me to wear what I wanted to wear. I have pictures of myself with three and four watches on at a time, and I do not know why, I suppose it was so sort of a healing process I had to go through.

My parents had always gone to church although; they did not attend every Sunday, they were members of a local church. I started attending church with them on a regular basis. My parents told me all the praying that had been done during my time at U.T. Hospital and I finally started to realize how grand GOD really is.

He can do ANYTHING. I finally began to realize all GOD had done for me. Not just for my family but, just for me. HE helped me learn to walk again plus, HE helped me to talk again. I needed to tell someone just about the Glorious things my GOD had done for me. I had always known that my Dad had been graced with a beautiful voice. So, I contacted a local church and I started singing about the way God had saved my soul. There was a reason that I was to keep on living it just was not my time to go yet. I believe everyone; all mankind has a time here in this world. That GOD has a plan for us all! With GODS help a person can move mountains and I believe this with all of my soul. Here I am with just a few scars on my arm and a very few on my hand and I do not have bad headaches, and it is all because of my GOD. HE did it all for me, and only me. And for all those who do not believe, I have a fear that they will wait until it is too late! I have a close relative who does not believe I pray that soon she and her family will wake up and see that GOD IS, WAS, and ALWAYS has been!

This world has many troubles going on right now and many people need GODS help. All whom believe need to help those who do not believe. In JESUS name AMEN! {**Author's Note**: I went to the church April started going to after the accident. My parents and her parents were friends. It's funny because her accident was several years before and much more serious than mine, but when I had my accident I thought of her. The doctor's told me mentally I might never get better, but I knew April had recovered and it gave me hope. I hadn't seen or spoken with April in about thirteen (13) years. When I was almost finished with the book God reminded me of April. My mom had stayed in touch with her and her family. My mom told me where April lived. I stopped by her house (no appointment or invitation) and told her what I was doing with this book and what I wanted from her. She graciously agreed to share her story and had it ready for me the very next day. I am thankful to God for her help. Even though I knew her story it still made me cry to read it. God is God and nothing is too big for God.}

I Got Real Sick
Rose, Johnnie –TN

I was saved at 15 years old and attended church regularly. I grew up and had a family.   When my children were growing up I worked to support them. I wanted to fulfill my role as a provider for my family but, I got real sick. I was put in the hospital for 2 and 3 weeks at a time. Three (3) different doctors thought I had a brain tumor. Some of the doctors wanted to lift my skull and do exploratory surgery on my brain. My family doctor did not agree to the brain surgery. He said because of the risk involved with the surgery and since I had a family he'd rather treat me with medication. They told me I would never be able to work again. I was on shots and medication for a long time. I One special night during church service I received a miracle! I felt as if I needed to be anointed and prayed for. The church did as such. To anoint means the church used oil (not because the oil had any healing powers and neither did the church, but just because we were being obedient to God's Holy word.) and knelt and prayed for me. I WAS HEALED INSTANTLY! I've was never again bothered with that sickness. I thank the Lord he took care of me! That was a miracle but God didn't stop there. There's so much God has done for me it'd be hard to tell it all. There was another time that God healed me. I had an ulcerated stomach. The doctor said I needed a very strict diet or surgery. My stomach was completely covered in sores. Again, I was prayed for at church. God again healed me instantly! Thank the Lord! To this day I am free from ulcers. I can eat anything I like without any problem. Thank the Lord!{**Author's Note**: I know many people don't believe in the anointing with oil. I really hadn't heard of it until a couple of years ago. I was in a church service one night and observed it being done. I went to my Bible and sure enough it does say to do that. We know the church doesn't have the power to heal, but almighty God does! The healing occurs through FAITH and obedience! The book of James 5:14-15 *"Is any sick among you? let him call for the elders of the church; and let them pray over him, anointing him with oil in the name of the Lord: And the prayer of FAITH shall save the sick, and the Lord shall raise him up; and if he have committed* *sins, they shall be forgiven him."* I attend church with Mr. Rose he truly enjoys the presence of the Lord. }

Prayer Changes Things
Smallwood, Gracie –VA

I'd always been pretty health not any serous health problems. I began to have some hurting in my chest. Just one small spot. It felt like a knot on a piece of wood. If you could just knock off that spot I would be fine. I went to the doctor and after an examination he wrote a prescription and told me I was having heart problems. When I took the prescription to the pharmacy the man that filled it old me he was sorry if was having such serious problems. I asked him why he said that. He told me that the medication was very powerful. The next time I went to church I went up for prayer. As I turned to go back to my seat I turned again to the pastor and told him I believed God healed me! He aid "Praise the Lord" The doctor learned again that God does heal. The doctor later became a Christian and was a good worker for the Lord.

The Cancer
Smallwood, Henry –VA

Not long after I gave my heart and back to Jesus I began to grow in the Lord and try to live close to God. I was happy in my walk with God. I loved the peace I had in my soul.

Shortly after something else wonderful happened. I got married. Everything seemed right with me now. But 11 months after our marriage I was diagnosed with throat cancer. I got up once morning big lump on the right side of my face. We went to the doctor. He never touched me in any way just looked in my mouth and said it was cancer. He made me an appointment to see a cancer doctor. Never once did I believe it was cancer. I know now it was.

I had two options. 1.) Surgery (so serious I would have had to have reconstructive surgery for my face. 2.) Radiation. Thru it all I did not believe it was cancer. I chose option 2. Many people were praying for me.

God healed me of the throat cancer! God healed me of this cancer and I know he healed me beyond all doubt. It will be time for my final doctor's appointment in October of 2006 and I will still be cancer free. My throat cancer is healed!

Other health issues have came up since then. My FAITH says God will keep on healing me, and taking care of me. I must say when they kept telling me it was cancer, I kept the FAITH. I believed and trusted that God would heal me. God will take great care of you too if you have FAITH. I thank God for his love for me and all my FAITH and trust is in him. My FAITH can not fail for I believe in the saving God whose hand I am in. {**Author's Note**: Henry is my grandfather. Most of the time he's busy telling jokes and having fun, but he's serious when it comes to his Lord.}

My Grandson
Tharp, Doris -TN (Written February 2006)

My grandson was two (2) years old. He had been sick off and on since birth. We were once told he had restricted airways disease. His fingernails were turning black and looked like they were rotten and would fall off. About six (6) months ago he was very sick for three (3) weeks straight. The doctor was testing him for Cystic Fibrosis a very serious disease that would not let him live, but maybe into his teens. God spoke to me and ask me to call upon the elders of the church. I called them and asked them to meet us at the church to pray for James (my grandson.) That night my husband and I took James to the church. He was burning up with fever and was just lifeless. I felt the spirit of God moving before we ever got in the church. The elders anointed him with oil and started praying and the Holy Spirit moved upon my grandson and at that moment he was healed! (We was waiting for the test results at this time.) James immediately began to get better! You could just see him getting better as we stood and talked. He was down playing in the parking lot before we ever left the church. He had no more fever! The doctor called the next day to tell me the test was negative. This was no surprise to me because God had moved while we were at church! There are times we all get sick and must face things. Whatever was wrong James the doctor healed him completely. He will still have to face things and sickness in his life, but God forever healed that illness. Thank You God!

The Addiction
Tharp, Doris -TN

Around six (6) years ago I was in a lot of pain in my legs and even had trouble walking. I went from one doctor to another and all would tell me the same "rheumatoid arthritis". I was put on different pills that did nothing. The pain was so unbearable the doctor told me all that was left to do was to go on a strong pain pill. I refused this for two (2) years because my father died at the age of fifty-four (54) with a massive heart attack and an addiction to pain medication. I did not want this for myself. I finally gave in. I couldn't stand the pain any longer. I started on Hydrocodone 10 milligram. It worked for a couple of years then it seemed not to help. The doctor then put me on a morphine patch plus the pain pill. I only used the patch a few months. I winged myself off that habit with the pain pills. It got to where two (2) pills was not enough. It came to the point where I had to have a pill to get up, two (2) or three (3) during the day, and a pain pill plus a sleeping pill to go to sleep. This went on for maybe three (3) years. I would pray for God to take this from me. At the same time I would justify my addition by saying the doctor has me on these medication and I must need them. Then one night my husband and daughter told me how all this medication had changed me. They told me I was not the same person I was before. I told them they was crazy. I needed my medication. By this time I was taking six (6) to eight (8) pills per day. I tried to justify taking the pills. I knew I had an addiction. I would pray for God's help. Then one morning around 05:00 A.M. I was in bed and I heard someone call my name. I opened my eyes to find no one in the room. I tried to go back to sleep. I heard my name called again. I looked again and there was no one around. The voice was there again this time it was just my name. He told me to take all my medication from my home. My husband was already gone to work. When he called my name the third (3rd) time he said if I didn't do as he said I would battle this addiction the rest of my life. I took the medication to my husband at his job. My husband had not been saved at this time. He told me I couldn't do this. The doctor had told us if I quit all at once I could die. I told him that God had spoke to me and told me. I told my husband it would be alright since God said it. My husband put the pills in his truck just in case is what he said. If you ever knew anyone coming off drugs you know the side effects (Pain, throwing up, and it can be really bad because I have seen my dad like this). God had shown me I would be ok. I had no withdrawals!

I've been off this medication for four (4) years. I was off the medication for almost a year before I realized God didn't only take the addiction but, he also took the pain that started this addiction. I had only been off the pain pills for about six (6) months when I took a sever headache that ended me up in the emergency room. The doctor was going to give me a shot of pain medication. This upset me and my husband explained to the doctor about my prior addiction. I thank God for a God fearing doctor. God gave him the words to say to me. The doctor said "God doesn't do anything halfway. If he healed you from addiction he will not let me suffer from addiction again." I took the shot and go rid of the headache.

I've had four (4) surgeries since that time and had to take some pain medication. I don't worry any more that I will ever get addicted again. God did heal me from addiction. He showed me that there may be times that I need pain medicine, but he will take care of me.

Multiple Sclerosis
Wallace, Rozella –TN

When my oldest son was born he was born with multiple sclerosis. The doctors said he would have to be on medication all of his life. I was heart broken. For here my first born was sick and I couldn't do anything for him. He would be sitting around playing and pass out. He hit his head many times, broke his teeth, cut his little chin, and all I could do was cry. My dad used to say "Why would God put a child through that for? It would be better if that child was dead" Well that really broke my heart. It broke my heart for my child being sick but most of all for my dad saying that. You see my dad didn't believe in God at that time. So one day I was along and very sad over things and the way my life was going. I started to pray. Just a short prayer I thought to ask God "why my child had to suffer so? When I got to talking to God it turned out to be for quite a while. I ask God to please help my baby, if it was his will let him get better and have to be sick or crippled for the rest of his life. When I took him back to the doctor he said "I believe he'll out grow this and may not have to take medication for the rest of his life. Well "Praise God" He didn't need the medication! God healed him. He's now grown and has three boys of his own. So don't let anyone tell you that God is dead or there's no God, I know better. Praise God today, tomorrow, and forever! Amen!

By the way, before my dad died he made it right with God. That's two (2) miracles God gave me. Thank God!

Seizures
Williams, Brenda –TN

The Lord can do all things. He is the way and the only way. Long years ago I was a very sick young lady. At the age of eighteen I had seizures very bad. The doctor said I would have to take seizure pills for the rest of my life. They put me on four pills a day, but let me tell you I had a higher doctor that sow a better way – no pills! The seizures were so bad that I would be out for days not knowing anything or anyone around me. Things changed for me later in the. The higher doctor came to me one night in church. At the church where I belong there was special worship meeting, let me tell you the Lord was there. The preacher was preaching on FAITH and healing. It was my time to let the Lord take care of me. The Lord came to me and said just come to me, have FAITH, and believe in being healed from your seizures. The power of the Lord was so strong I had to go up and have the FAITH that the Lord was going to heal me. The best feeling came over me that I ever had. I know that God healed me that night right there in the little church. Let me tell you that Lord can do all things. We the people just have to have FAITH and believe in him. Let me tell you the Devil is a liar. The Devil tries to tell me that God didn't heal me, that I would see - that I would have another seizure. That's where FAITH comes in, because we know that God don't lie. Let me tell you I am seizure free! Healed! The Lord healed me from this sickness. No doctors, No pills, God! I have to say I thank God for healing me from this, but most of all is being able to say I am his. That's the best testimony to me. I hope this helps someone with having FAITH. There are a lot of things I don't understand but I know that God is real and he is alive today and forever more. {**Author's Note**: I attend church with Brenda. This testimony is truly a FAITH builder.}

FAITHful Obedience
Williams, Jackie –TN

I'd been having problems in my neck. It was so bad I couldn't stand it. It went on for about two (2) years. This little old lady wanted the church to pray for her. The Lord came to me and said "if you want your neck to be healed sit down there." I said Lord I don't want to take anything away from her. I want to be praying for her. He come back to me and said "I got plenty there's nothing short about me. If you want to be healed just sit down." I obeyed the Lord and sat down and had the church pray for me to. My neck is better. I thank God for healing that. This is my testimony the best that I could give it. I hope that this will reach someone out there in someway, that they may take and give their life to the Lord. If your backslid on the Lord I beg you to go back to the church and work for God.

Thyroid Cancer
Williams, Rosella –TN

One day I was having pain in my side. I had lost a lot of weight. I went to the doctor he didn't know what it was so he sent me to have some test. The doctor there was worried why I had lost weight and they kept doing more test. Then he sent me to a surgical doctor. They were checking to see if it was my thyroid. They did a biopsy. I had two (2) knots in my neck. He said the only way he would do surgery was if it bothered me. I told him that it was. He put me in the hospital and done surgery. When I went back for my check up I had Thyroid cancer. He said where it was they would never have found it if I hadn't had surgery. Thank the Lord for letting them find it. That was four (4) years ago and I am cancer free. See what you don't know is my husband asked the church to pray for me and my sickness. My brother died from Thyroid cancer, but through FAITH I am healed!

Her Feet Were Healed
Wood, Thelma "Ruth" - TN(Lovingly written down by her daughters Vickie Graves & Debbie Muncey)

In October 2000, our mom Thelma "Ruth" Wood was having problems with her feet and legs. She was a diabetic an on dialysis due to kidney failure. Her toes was getting blisters on them, when they would bust her toes would turn black. She was sent to a specialist, on October 24, 2000. He told us that mom had very little blood circulation from the knees down in both legs. On November 21, 2000 mom had to have her middle toe removed from her left foot. The doctor told us to take mom home let her have a good Thanksgiving and Christmas, then return to his office on January 16, 2001. He told us that he would then take both legs from the knee down. Prayers started from different churches and people for mom. We were so upset and worried about mom, but she didn't seem to be worried, she had FAITH that God would take care of it. When we took mom back to the doctor he was amazed that her feet were healed. We told him about the prayers and he (the doctor) said that it was a miracle. We lost mom on November 11, 2003 due to fluid build up that dialysis couldn't control. She went peacefully to be with her Lord. {**Author's Note**: Psalms 75:1 says this: *Unto thee, O God, do we give thanks, unto thee do we give thanks: for that thy name is near thy wondrous works declare.*}

He Will Be Here
Wood, Tony – TN (Lovingly written in memory by Vicki Graves)

The miracle for Tony Wood started on November 11, 2002. On this date he went to the hospital with trouble breathing. While in the emergency room he stopped breathing and had to be shocked. He suffered many strokes which resulted in the loss of his eyesight and his left side. He also lost feeling in both hands. He was in intensive care for 51 days. The doctors told us that he would never be able to walk, talk, or breath on his own. He would be a vegetable. Tony was a fighter and with God's will he left the hospital as his own. In April 2003, Tony had another problem breathing; we took him to another hospital. While there Jason Dyer (A local preacher) would visit. One time Jason called an told us to tell Tony that he wasn't coming that night but would if he needed him. We told Tony this and he said "he will be here". To our surprise Jason walks in later. That was the night that Tony received Jesus as his Saviour. Tony went through a lot of doctor and therapy trying to restore his sight. We made many trips to Nashville, Georgia, and Knoxville. Tony was depressed and wanted to give up. He told me that he wouldn't go to Heaven if he took his own life. With love, prayers, and FAITH we had Tony until December 30, 2004. We was waiting for the other miracle, for Tony to get his sight back. We know that he now can see! {**Author's Note**: We may not always understand everything that happens, but God has a purpose for all things.}

What is a Miracle?
Woodward, Rochester J. – VA

A miracle is "an effect in the physical world which surpasses all known human or natural powers and is therefore ascribed to supernatural agency. A marvel! A wonder!" Perhaps many people know the word, "miracle", but has never seen one. We've seen and had many "miracles" in our families, but today, I only want to focus on just one and that's the miracle in my life! My name is Rochester J. Woodward and I live in a small community called Stone Creek. This is three (3) miles from the town of Pennington Gap, Virginia. I grew up in a Christian family with my father (an evangelist) my mother (a powerful prayer warrior and a complement to my father.) Both had "miracles" in their lives. They knew a wonderful man called "Jesus" and believed with all their hearts just how powerful prayer was and told me and all my brothers and sisters that "Jesus was always there with us – just a whisper away!" We grew up in church so we knew a lot about miracles and just who cold perform miracles! Some of us were saved at a very young age and others later in life. We all knew who "Jesus" was and that he was real, alive, and gave mankind hope. When there wasn't any hope before "Jesus" came on the scene dying for you and me!

Let me tell you a little about what took place before that wonderful day came that I received my miracle. It was a beautiful June day with the temperature being about seventy (70) degrees. It was clear and sun shiny. My wife Clair woke me up very early on this particular day. Though I'd worked the second (2nd) shift ant Tennessee Eastman Company in Kingsport, Tennessee. She was excited about receiving our video movie camera we had ordered. We had one child at that time and we wanted to take pictures of our daughter, Michelle, who was eight (8) months old. I hurriedly dressed in a pair of Bermuda shorts and shower shoes. I needed to go just below our home to a Gas Station to turn in my rental uniforms to get new clean ones. I told my wife I'd return shortly.

As I entered the front door of the station no one was present even though it was 10:30 A.M. The front office was empty. I placed my uniforms on the floor where the rental company had a pickup station. Leaving there I proceeded to the bay area where cars are greased and maintenance done underneath the cars. There was a recessed ramp, a pit down below the normal floor of the garage square in shape where the service attendant works underneath the vehicles. Sometimes grease cans and old soiled rags were lying around beneath their feet as they worked. Hazardous! Yes! I heard and seen men working in the pit. I walked over, bent down, and looked into the pit. Before anything was said all of a sudden there was a loud terrifying bang. Flamers were everywhere! In the pit, above the pit, the men and I were all consumed in flames. Skin burnt clothes on fire and for a brief moment in shock as to what had happened. Located in the bottom of the pit was the sub pump which arched igniting the gas and hazardous fumes causing an explosion and the fire. The blast was so strong it shook houses near by. I knew I was burnt severely but with the help of the Lord and God's mercy he helped me have the strength to get up. Even though I felt my skin on fire, skin burnt to a crisp, skin drawing and beginning to wrinkle and shrink I made my way across the highway to a store/restaurant knowing someone there could help me. As I stumbled on my way to get help the first thing that I thought of and about of all things was about chickens. I remembered when I was a little boy we'd take chickens, kill them, and would single them over an open fire to remove all feathers that were left after we plucked out all we could. Then the "fire" did the rest. That's how I felt. I was alive! I felt the fire through my body.

It was burning just like we'd done to those chickens, but they felt nothing! I felt everything.

As I approached the store/restaurant I knew it was only by God's mercy that I could walk. I as reached the door I realized that I couldn't open the door. It was only at that time I was startled to see that all flesh had been blown off both my hands! Burned off! I saw a little boy riding a bicycle coming my way and I stopped him to see if he'd open the door for me. He did and I walked in. There was an elderly man sitting there he saw that I needed help and came toward me. I asked if he'd take me to the Hospital and he quickly assisted me. The ride was only three miles away but was one of the longest rides I'd ever experienced. I knew deep down I was almost burned alive! Only God's grace and mercy had spared me from this terrible tragedy! Even though I was severely burned I never lost consciousness. I always knew my surroundings and that I needed medical attention. The elderly man drove me to the emergency room and I walked in on my own arms and hands out stretched. The nursed saw me black and burnt to a crisp! They immediately laid me on the floor and began putting ice all over my body. I was completely packed in ice and only my eyes were seen. No skin whatsoever was spared by the fire except for a small section of hair on my head! Hideous for anyone to look upon! More like a character in a horror film.!

I was burned so badly this hospital didn't have the facilities at that time they said to care for such a degree of burn as this was and that I needed to be transferred to another hospital not far way that treated burned patients. The doctors/nurses did what they could for me for three (3) hours and then I was transferred to another hospital about and hour away. This was another agonizing drive, but hoping help, relief, and comfort was awaiting me there. I went by ambulance to the other hospital. Before Leaving I was placed in a bed and the nurses removed all the ice from my body except for my arms which still had packs. My flesh felt as if the fire had begun all over again. The pain was unbearable! Excruciating pain! Suffering beyond belief! The ice melted on my arms even before we arrived at our destination. The pain worsened! I was still conscious during all this time and experiencing every pain since the first minute of impact at the gas station. Not any medication relieved my ordeal.

My wife and family were notified by this time and by my side. My face was so horrible. I asked the nurses to put towels over my face so it wouldn't scare/shock my wife seeing how badly I was burned. Even though I was in terrible pain I wanted to try to protect my family from knowing the worse and what may happen! My dad rode in the ambulance with me. I didn't want my wife to see just how much pain I was in. For her sake I asked her if she'd ride with my mother and they could comfort each other. Praying was my mother's main and only source in getting in touch with God and her request be known no matter the situation. She went straight to the Throne of God. My wife wasn't a Christian at that time, either. As the pain continued to get worse by the minute I asked my dad to just open the door of the ambulance and jump out. I felt as though I was dying and since we were traveling over high and dangerous mountains this would be a way to put an end to my suffering! Death had never entered my mind until now. How much suffering could a person take before wanting to put an end to life? For at this point, life didn't seem worth living! This appeared to be the best way out of a bad situation – take my own life. My dad said no! That's not what anyone wanted for me especially God! Jumping would have put an end to all this suffering and I couldn't think of anything else at this point. It was an excruciating pain clouding my mind.

I wasn't a born again Christian at this time so praying myself was out of the question. Even though I'd seen prayer come to past I was empty inside and couldn't call upon the Lord Jesus. It seemed I was alone with no where to turn except take this pain and put an end to my life. My dad was a praying man among all men. He was a great dad! He was very quiet, loved by his family, and he knew how to get in touch with God! People knew my parents were Christians even before they told anyone. It showed! God was in their! God was their life! My dad was small in stature. When he prayed for me this time he looked ten (10) feet tall. His voice sounded as thunder. I am positive if it had been heard on the outside of the ambulance people would have accepted the Lord as their Saviour. They would have thought this voice rang out as though it came down from Heaven. My dad may have been called a mountain man called by God, but to meet him you knew where he was coming from. Who he was all about and his purpose in life! He wanted to see souls saved for the kingdom of God.

We eventually arrived at the hospital. God's mercy was still with me. I couldn't believe it but I was still alive. I knew with all the prayers going up it couldn't have happened any other way. God is FAITHful to those who are FAITHful to him. I knew my parents were FAITHful and devoted to the Lord! I was admitted and taken to my room. My family was informed that with the degree of burns I had patients didn't always survive. If I made it through the night it would be a small chance I'd pull through. The doctors ordered Morphine and other strong drugs for me but to no avail. Relief was no where to be seen or felt. Still conscious never going to sleep or getting any relief my pain continued to get worse. If that was possible. It was so bad I really wanted to die just to escape this terrible pain. God pulled me through another day and night for he knew he had a plan for me and this wasn't' going to be the end of the road for me. This was just the beginning, but I didn't know all that yet.

Early the next morning we got the report that I had been burned seventy (70%) from the top of my head to the top of my feet. I still had some skin on my buttocks and the bottom of my feet. The rest was beyond recognition. This was first, second, and third degree burns! Flesh all gone from my hands, and my face was split open from the blast of the explosion coming up and hitting me directly in the face. My back and chest was burned so badly the doctors told my family that my kidneys probably would not function. My legs on the inside of my knees had huge holes blown out as well as no skin on them. Softballs could have been placed in seventy (70%) percent of my body in many places for there were such deep blown out flesh. Flesh consumed by fire is a terrible thing for anyone, especially for the victim who can still smell the burning of flesh and have that odor all around you and knowing that it is coming form your body! A smell never forgotten! Yet God's grace is sufficient! More than enough. I laid there in terrible pain. I knew God continued to let me breathe and be alive under those circumstances. At times, I would even wonder why? My doctor treated severe burn patients. He was in World War II. He told me and my family that I looked like some of the soldiers he had treated in the war who had been burned by jet fuel. The doctor was very blunt, but believed the patient should know what to expect in these conditions. He said that I was charred like a black marshmallow and that the head from the blast had to have been between 2800 – 3500 degrees F. Very extreme heat! Hot! With all the medication, tubes, and machines nothing eased my pain. The pain was constantly with me it never diminished. I was wrapped in ice and some kind of soiled treated wraps. I looked like an Egyptian mummy. My body began to blister after a while. Big bags of water formed in these huge blisters. My head swelled as big as a basketball. Nothing ever helped me no matter what they did. The doctors kept giving me more and more Morphine hoping for relief but it never came.

I was told my future looked very bleak. If I had anything to look forward to at all it was that during the next year I'd still be in the hospital. I could be handicapped in some ways when leaving there. Maybe the kidneys would have to be put on a kidney machine. Perhaps the skin grafts wouldn't take not to mention all the medication I'd have to take all my life. I could lose some control of the usage in my hands or legs. So many things to think about even before my pain could be put under control. The doctors were always worried about me getting pneumonia, germs, and infection. In which I wasn't or couldn't have fought off any of these things had they happened. God stepped in and by his mercy none of the bad possibilities happened. As I mentioned before my dad was a praying man. We had miracles to take place in our family so he knew this was nothing too big for his God to take care of! Everyone in my family began calling around the area and out of the area to ask for prayer for me. They knew Christians that could get in touch with God. Prayers were going up in homes, churches, and even on T.V. They knew this would be just another miracle somewhere down the road that the Lord Jesus would perform. There were distant relatives in my family who were very skeptical. They were having doubts as well as showing doubts that God could heal me! You could hear some saying "there's no way that Rochester would pull through this tragedy! It won't happen because he is too far gone wit all the seventy (70%) percent burns he has!" When it seems impossible that's when God makes it possible to happen! With so much pain and never any relief there just wasn't' any rest for my soul! I more thane ever wanted to die! I couldn't live this way and it seemed as if this would be my life forevermore. Who would want to live in such agony and have so much inner unrest? This wasn't living! This was physical death for I was already spiritually dead! I couldn't do anything about either one. That's what I thought in my weak state of mind! The enemy doesn't want us to know the way to a better peaceful life or that Jesus is the way the truth and the life.

Yes, I was a lost soul who could not concentrate for a second about Hell or Heaven! My dear mother would talk to me and say "Pray Rochester! Pray!" There was no prayer coming from my lips. I just couldn't pray. I tried and tried. Why couldn't I pray? I wondered? What was wrong with me? I knew there was a living God and he could heal me and he could save me! What was the problem? Still unable to pray on the third (3rd) day I was taken to physical therapy where a crane lifted me into a big pool of water – a whirlpool! They let me just soak for hours then I'd be lifted out to sit in a chair to dry. Then they would strip the burned skin from my body. That just added more pain to me. The therapist told my wife that I never once screamed or cried out when the skin was being torn away. He said "your husband is a very strong person for we have never had anyone come through here that didn't cry, scream, or begged to have us quit" he also said "Your husband must have something on the inside in order to withstand all that he's going through on the outside" This treatment was done everyday. Nothing to look forward to.

My wife and mother come over that third (3rd) day to see me as they did everyday. They couldn't stay with me because there were three (3) other burnt patients in that room and this was a male ward. My brother, Jerry, came down from Indiana and stayed with me at night. He was so much help to me and I appreciated his sacrifice he was doing for me. My family was always there in the day time, but had to leave at night. Everyone who come up to the floor could smell "burnt flesh" as they stepped off the elevator. I was so deformed and horrible looking even some of the men in my family couldn't bear to look at me. My wife was always there loving me and taking care of me. She never bothered with how I looked! True love can over look any situation and make it seem normal and just another day caring for her loved ones. My mother had prayed all night and she said that God had given her a scripture for me. It was the Psalms 116:1-19. She read all the Psalms to me as follows: "Love the Lord, because he hath heard my voice and my supplications. Because he hath inclined his ear unto me, therefore will I cal upon him as long as I live. The sorrows of death compassed me and the pains of hell got hold upon me; I found trouble and sorrow. Then called I upon the name of the Lord; O Lord, I beseech thee deliver my soul. Gracious is the Lord and righteous; yeah, our God is merciful. The Lord preserveth the simple: I was brought low and he helped me. Return unto my rest, O my soul; for the Lord hath dealth bountifully with thee. For thou has delivered my soul from death, mine eyes from tears and my feet from falling. I will walk before the Lord in the land of the living. I believed, therefore have I spoken: I was greatly afflicted. I said in my haste all men are liars. What shall I render unto the Lord for all his benefits toward me. I will take the cup of salvation and call upon the name of the Lord. I will pray my vows unto the Lord now in the presence of all his people. Precious in the sight of the Lord is the death of his saints. O Lord, truly I am thy servant; I am thy servant and the son of thine handmaid; thou has loosed my bonds. I will offer to thee the sacrifice of thanksgiving and will call upon the name of the Lord. I will pay my vows unto the Lord now in the presence of all his people. In the courts of the Lord's house in the midst of the, O Jerusalem, praise ye the Lord. After the reading of Gods word my cold-stone heart was crushed! Tears began to flow like a river – unstoppable@ It was at this moment I knew God was calling me to repentance. That beautiful day I accepted Jesus as my Saviour. I was born into his kingdom a child of the living God.

At that very moment this huge heavy mountain that seemed to have weighted me down had been lifted off my shoulders. Everyone heard praying day and night coming from my room. As I called on Jesus that third (3rd) floor hospital knew that something had happened and someone had touched Jesus. It was in the air and on the faces of everyone in my room and on that floor. Even though I was now happy in my heart and soul my physical pain was still very read and unbearable as ever. It was at this time I knew Jesus would make it easier to bear and he did. The strenuous treatments continued every day and this time I knew God's mercy and grace for me and with me through these trying times. On the seventh day doctors informed my wife and family that I would have to have surgery (skin grafts) done. The wanted to prepare us because sometimes skin grafts didn't take. They needed to get blood donors for me which wasn't a problem because even the nursed in the hospital volunteered to give blood. Some skin on my body would have to be used for skin grafts to my face, arms, back and legs. The doctors were concerned about the large open holes in my legs. I was told some of the skin on my buttocks and the bottom of my feet could be used in the skin grafts. Which seemed like such a small amount of skin to have cover my body and fill the holes in my legs. My family had FAITH that everything would be alright. All the following days everything was getting set for the surgery. My days were filed with people sitting by my bedside praying for me. It was like a sweet smell over coming the smell of my burnt flesh.

I had recently accepted the Lord as my Saviour, I hadn't had a lot of time to grow with the Lord and since I was so weak I hate to admit this, but anger rose up in me each time my pain kept getting worse. I hated to see the days and nights come. Though the Lord comforted my heart during these times and his mercy was right there with me it was a difficult time. Such a loving and forgiving God! To let me still be alive with my family and friends. All the brothers/sisters from very denomination lifting me up to the Lord. They had all come together for just one purpose and that was for me! To intervene on my behalf! On day ten (10) my wife had gotten everyone together for the preparation day of the surgery. Many people where there to assist in whatever way they could. This was just another day starting out like every day before or at least I thought it was. My routine of having someone roll me to therapy, picking me up on a crane, lowering me into the pool of water and just soaking. After a few hours I was lifted out of the pool and placed in my wheel chair and taken back to my room to dry out. This took almost three (3) hours before the doctor came to see me. He said that he'd come to prepare me for surgery. Remembering that day now seems like it was only yesterday.

The doctor was a religious man in the sense of being a Christian and had taken forceps in his hand to remove some of the burnt skin. He first looked at the holes in my legs and next to the lowest part began pulling the black skin off. He finished the leg and went to my other leg pulling more skin away. He didn't say anything to me, but looked up as if he was astonished, but continued on. I didn't know what to expect. Was this a good look or bad look on his face? At that moment he quit looked up and me and said "Son, I don't know if you believe in God or not, but if you do, this would be a great time to start thanking him for what he's done and is doing for you." He said "I see knew skin under the black burnt skin and it's like a newborn babies skin! As the doctor continued to examine other parts of my body where the skin grafts would have taken place he told me that there were new baby skin there also. All of the skin that had been burned was now being replaced with new skin! He said that I wouldn't have to have skin grafts. No surgery, but reminded me and he family that I was still in critical danger. The doctor commented to us that there were many doctors in that hospital with many religious beliefs and if I believed what my God had done give him praise and glory and thank him for what he's doing. Evidently when I accepted the Lord as my Saviour the doctor had the day off and didn't hear the good news. The doctor carried a King James Bible in his white coat pocket. It could be seen about the opening pocket. The doctor was a doctor among and above doctors for he knew the Lord Jesus for himself. Today it's very unusual to find doctors that are Christians. That was a rejoicing day for all of us! Just knowing that God put new skin where there wasn't any! Can you imagine? What a miracle! Only God could do that! Even the doctor experienced a miracle through me. A wonderful happy day in my life that will never be forgotten and I will always tell this miracle for the rest of my life. God is so good!

According to the doctors I still had a dangerous road ahead. Large blisters bigger than your hands began to appear covering my body. The pain began again even worse than before. It was unbearable! Fever set in! My temperature went to 105 degrees every evening. I felt has though this could be just a little like Hell and I was right in the middle of it. Not only that but it seemed like a voice was telling me to just die and get this ordeal over with. Those that don't know about that deceiving voice it belongs to our enemy, the devil. He wants us to fail when we find the Lord just deny God and die! That's not God's plan for us! When God opens the windows of blessings Satan opens the doors of sabotage!

My oldest brother Joe, was in the army in North Caroling. Joe was a Christian and powerful prayer warrior. He was called about my situation. Joe cam in to be with us. First he headed above our home in the mountains to pray. My dad had an alter made there in the forest of trees and rocks and we as children and even grown-ups would go with our dad to pray and seek God there. Joe prayed all night there at that alter by himself and with God naturally. As morning came he returned to mother's house and told her what took place while praying for me. Joe said "mom, as I was praying for Rochester it seemed like I was looking through a huge tunnel. At the end of the tunnel I could see a small light. God assured him that I would be ok and not to worry any more.

Joe came to the hospital and prophesied to me that by July 4th I would be home with my family celebrating the holiday at home. He said I'd be eating ice cream and watermelon with everyone. There were skeptics who didn't believe and even couldn't understand how that would be possible in my condition. I kept hearing the doctors say I'd be there six (6) months to a year. Deep down on the inside I knew that my God could do anything. There's nothing too big for him. Look how he gave me new baby skin! God made this body so repairing a few parts here and there wasn't a big problem for him. Just the lift of his little finger or a thought could put me back together again.

With all the blisters hanging from my body therapy was again taken place as usual. When more and more skin was stripped away this felt like a terrible nightmare! As they began to strip off the old skin I thought this shouldn't be happening to a human being. It was beyond unbearable. At this time I did scream out loud or silently I wasn't sure. When I was in the water and flesh was torn away from my body. It didn't' help to scream, but perhaps it would stomp out the ache of the pain. The therapist said I was still the best strongest patient ever – very brave! Returning to my room I had to lay still while I dried. My wife would peel the black crust off my face and body. She did this every day that I was in the hospital. She looked at me as though nothing was wrong! She was always by my side encouraging me, feeding me, reading tome or to give a little pat of affection on my shoulder letting me know everything was going to be fine and discharge from the hospital was just around the corner. The nurses still kept giving me Morphine and more Morphine. This bothered me since I didn't know a lot about the medication at the time. I was told it was addictive. I didn't want to become an addict by taking this drug which didn't help anyway. I cancelled the Morphine and refused to take anymore. The pain was still there trying to get the best of me. This was when I became tired of being defeated by the devil and started praying with everything in me t call upon the Lord to help take this terrible pain away. It seemed within minutes that my prayer along with my families that God answered and gave me some relief. I could feel the sharp pains being lifted away. The pain that was lift Jesus made it possible for me to bear. I knew he would take all my pain away, but it was in his time and not mine. How I appreciated the little things in my life at that particular time. Each day was exactly like the day before. Stripping flesh from my body by wife and therapist. This was just another routine day for me. To look upon me most people would have thought I looked like an ugly monster not human at all. Something began to happen on this particular day. My condition had began to improve. This amazed al my doctors for I had eight (8) doctors in all. Not a big change but enough for the doctors to come and prepare for the future according to them.

The doctors said I'd never get to be out in the sunshine because of my tender baby skin. Being around heat was out of the question. To have full use of my hands and legs was very slim and the kidneys were left in question also. I was a certified pipe welder so how would I support my family if I couldn't use my hands? These things kept going through my mind. Then something arose in my spirit. My mind was at ease and my outlook for life became clear. I realized that everything was in God's hand and that all these things were small compared to my Big God and al the big great and wonderful things that he could miraculously do. I didn't get discouraged after that because I had survived. I had my family by my side and I had Jesus living I me. My future was in his hands – not mine. After coming to this marvelous understanding and having so much peace within me, even the every day routines weren't as bad. Don't get me wrong pain was still around.

On the third (3rd) day of July the doctor entered my room closed the curtains surrounding my bed and said to me "We have discussed you case as it is and now we truly believe that we can let you go home tomorrow to see if you can make it living at home. Though our time period was set for a lot longer. We want to discharge you tomorrow! Some of the doctors didn't understand why I was going home early, but we all did! Tomorrow being the 4th of July, "rang a bell" as the prophesy my brother gave me back in June had come true! I would be home with everyone celebrating one of the best 4th of July's ever. Just before the doctor left he turned to me and said " always remember that your God brought you through so much and gave you something that burnt patients usually don't get, and that was new skin. God did your surgery! So place your trust in him because there is nothing we have done to make you will. It was a miracle" He told me to come back if I needed to otherwise there's nothing else they could do. He said "God is taking care of ;your new skin, he's filling in the holes in your legs, and taking your pain away. That he was sure my kidneys would be taken care of also. This is part of the miracle of creating a new creature. That's a miracle among miracles!" I knew God would take care of all my problems and he did!

On the fourth (4th) of July I was eating some good food and enjoying ice cream and watermelon like a small excited child at my parents home with family and friends. Everyone was happy to see me there and knowing they had seen a miracle.

I was very weak and had to learn to walk again. I couldn't use my hands very well at first and it reminded me of a baby trying to focus or cooperate for the first time with their hands. The only clothes I could wear were Bermuda shorts and flip flops for now. Day by day I could see improvements on my body and movements.

My wife continued to feed me for the next two (2) months. She was my special nurse. Never leaving my side. She was always with me. Being home with her and my little daughter was really good medicine. My new flesh (skin) began to seep over my burned body from the top of my head to my feet. My hair grew back in thicker than ever. I could get outside in the sun without burning and heat didn't harm me. Al things I was told by the doctors didn't take place. When my God does something it's always done right and done perfectly! This was an unfortunate accident with a miraculous ending. This happened in June and in October I returned to my job – welding!

I was completely healed! I have no scars! I have no after effects, no holes in my legs, my hands were as normal as before. To look at me no one would have believed I was burned until I told them my testimony! I have skin without a flaw! No one could tell I was burned because they couldn't see where God's surgery took over. I was completely made who by the power of God!

I know there's definitely nothing impossible with God! Just take a look at me! God made a new creature out of me in many ways. He saved me, cleansed me and gave me a miracle that I can tell wherever I go. Good news! If I have to go to a doctor for an examination it gives me a chance to tell them and those around about being burned to a crisp, but I came out smelling like a rose and not burnt skin. That God did a miracle in my life! I love him will all my heart! He took dead burned flesh and made a living miracle – brand new skin!

My wife experienced this miracle with me and it wasn't long before she also accepted the Lord! It's wonderful having a Christian home. We have a Saviour who is always there with us and true believers that surround us. Every day with the Lord is worth living! How about you? Is there a miracle awaiting you? {**Author's Note**: What a miracle! The thing that touches my heart most is his family. Doesn't this just show us how precious a Godly family is.}

The Light
Name Withheld – TN

I was very sick. I had been the hospital for many days. I had to have an IV to continue my medication, but my veins weren't very good. I was told that it was because I had been in there such a long time and with the constant vomiting (about 2 weeks of it) my veins just couldn't take much more. I remember they had to find a good vein and reinsert my IV. This seemed like an impossible task. They tried in spot and when they were digging for the vein they hit my bone! I will never be able to describe the pain. It was without a doubt the worst pain I have ever felt! I have felt the pain of giving birth, the after pains, had route canals, etc. None of those compare to the pain I felt when they hit my bone. Mentally I've always thought myself to be a pretty strong person, but that was more than I could handle. The nurses and doctors told my mom I had "a fit". They said I went into a rage. This in itself was a miracle because I wasn't healthy enough to say a whole lot. They called my mom in to calm me down. She begged they are going to try again they have to. I knew what she meant. I was vomiting every few minutes (even though the only substance on my stomach was the liquid food they were feeding me.) if I didn't get my IV I would die. I wasn't living for God, but I had been saved. I began to beg God "Please, God, Please just let this be ok." "Please God, Please just let them get the needle in and not hit my bone." I prayed over and over within my heart as they came back to attempt this again. The nurse came over and you could see how nervous she was. I think she was kind and was terrified of hurting me again. She couldn't find a good vein she started to call for help and then it happened. While I was praying I looked out the window of my hospital room. This beautiful glowing light shown through the window onto my arm. When that light (my Jesus) hit my arm she found a good vein. Not only that she got it in. It didn't even hurt when she put the needle in. What's more than that is that I had to be in there a few more days and I never needed another IV. God not only healed my veins and let me get that IV without pain, but he healed my entire illness. God healed me completely! Even more than that I've always had the kind of veins that roll so sick or not they used to have a hard time sticking me. Do you know that since that day (that was several years ago) I've never had trouble with my veins. God is a mighty God. Thank God for what he's done for me!

My Eyes
Name Withheld – TN

I had a severe eye infection. I had the infection for several months and never went to the doctor. It got so bad one Wednesday night that water was flowing from right eye just like a fountain. I could barely see to drive to church that night. I believe one of the deacons said something about being obedient. I knew what I had to do. I am stubborn and hate to ask for help, but I had to that night. I went to the front and asked the church to anoint me and pray for me. The fluid instantly stopped running from my eye and within a few days the infection was gone altogether. Thanks be to God!

CHAPTER 3

FAITH WORKED IT OUT!

**{2. Corinthians 5:7 (*For we walk by FAITH,
not by sight*)}**

My Sister's Story
Barnett, Jackie – VA (by Mildred Sparks)

This is my sister's testimony. When she was 18 months old she was very sick and in the hospital. They told us she was paralyzed and blind. They said she wouldn't live to be 6 months old. She was in the hospital for three months. They said when the medicine ran out she would die. Dad was at the hospital at the top of the stairs praying. There was an old white-headed man came up to him and ask him what was wrong. He told the man. The old man said let's just pray she'll be ok. Dad and the old man prayed. When dad opened his eyes the man was gone. Jackie lived! She was not paralyzed or blind!

Jackie wasn't exactly normal though they were a section of her brain that is dead. It will never mature beyond the age of eight. Just meeting Jackie and talking to her you can tell something is wrong but not what exactly. Jackie is now 54 years old.

She has read the Bible through 19 times. She can tell you how many books in the Bible. She knows the Bible very well. She is the only one of 11 kids that's never been married. We are all still living. I live here and take care of Jackie. She needs a little assistance.

I just wanted you to know we do believe in miracles because Jackie is one. By the help of God her condition is under control. Jackie is a Heaven sent child. My husband used to tell me that mom and dad was blessed. There's something she has the rest of us don't have. She sits constantly with her Bible. She reads the Bible all the time. She doesn't' watch anything on TV besides gospel stations and game shows. She's never watched a movie. She refuses. She is a blessing and a prayer warrior. I hope this will be a blessing to somebody somewhere along the way. Try if you will to imagine what it would be like to be in her shoes. {**Author's Note:** I've never met this woman, but you can feel the love of God in this testimony.}

May Christ Live in your Heart Always
Hodge, Jack - TN

Carrying the Cross is Rick Newton's passion, talking to people and seeing lives saved is what Rick is all about. Rick has traveled around the world with his 12 foot cross. Rick Newton is for real, A product of Gods Love And salvation. A quote from Rick, "Jesus called for all Christians to be fishers of men." Rick believes if one is going fishing, he must go where the fish are, in the fast-flowing streams and muddy pools of life.

I spent three and half-hours talking to Rick one evening. We met at Sissy's Country Kitchen on Newport Highway. Rick had just finished his day on the highway talking to any and all that would stop. You see, that is what Rick does, he walks the highways with his twelve foot cross. Talking to his fellow man about our Lord and Saviour Jesus Christ.

Rick was raised in Miami Florida, thrown out of his home in his mid-teens, and grew up among the hatred and violence of the 1960's. Rick spent the first 20 years of his life not believing in God. But, on June 10th 1972, Rick committed his life to Jesus Christ. Rick first shouldered the cross at the infamous House Of The Rising Son in New Orleans during Mardi Gras 1975. The owner of the House

Of The Risen Son had gotten saved in 1973. He said the Devil has had this place long enough, and turned it into The Bourbon Street Church.

Rick and a team had gone to New Orleans to witness for Jesus at Mardi Gras. They had been there about a week and things were going rough. One of the guys with Rick said something had to be done to get some attention, so he said lets build a 12-foot cross. The man was in his late 40s and Rick was 22, so the man said you are going to carry the Cross-Rick. When Rick walked out on the Bourbon Street with the cross. The response was immediate. Rick said The crowds parted like the red sea. Rick walked up Bourbon street preaching over a bullhorn.

When Rick left New Orleans he took the Cross back to San Antonio, Texas where he was directing a coffee house Ministry called His Place, they worked with the street gangs and bikers. The Cross-was hung on the wall of the Coffeehouse where it become a vocal point. Rick would take the Cross when he went out into the streets to witness to the street gangs and bikers. This was in the 1970's when there were open air concerts like Woodstock. Rick had asked if they could have 15 minutes and he was given the ok. Rick preached to 25,000 people from the stage that Sunday at a Rock Concert in San Antonio, Texas. They had a tent set up and were giving away water-melon. Rick invited anyone wanting to know more about Jesus to stop by the Jesus tent. When Rick took the cross on the road, after instructions from God to do so, he went to the Alamo to lead the Jesus marches. Then on to Colorado. Rick was Associate Pastor, Youth Director and Field Evangelist for a Church.

God spoke to Rick again to go on the road. His first country after going full time with the Cross was New Zealand where he carried the Cross the length of the Country, after he has been to Mexico, Guatemala, Salvador, Honduras, Nicaragua and around that area. Rick has carried his cross around the United States, into Canada, Central America, Europe, Africa, the Middle East, and the South Pacific. He has walked into coupes in Fiji and the Soviet Union and ministered to the Troops in the first Gulf War. Rick was arrested in Egypt, shot at in Jerusalem, had a rifle stuck in his face in El Salvador.

Rick was invited to pass out Bibles to the Government leaders inside the Kremlin in Moscow. While in Russia Rick passed out a total of 75,000 Bibles. Rick has been rained on, hailed on, blistered by the scorching sun and almost frozen while sleeping along the side of the road in Maine.

A message I received from Rick when he was in the Carolinas on his way to DC.:

Praise the Lord the message of the Cross is going forward. Seeing people saved, Tons of churches are committing to pray and fast July 4th week with me. Several coming to DC to help... NBC is trying to get with me right now to do an interview. They found out through papers I was in. All is going great here. People are stopping all the time giving me a chance to minister and pray with them. Last week I even got to share with a chain gang cleaning the road side along US Hwy 1 here in NC. The guard just stood there with his shotgun on his shoulder while I shared with the guys that Jesus loves them. Reminding them that Jesus died on the cross for each one of them. They received it well...I even had a pastor walk with me a little and really open up and share some struggles in his life. Some real honesty there. A lady pulled over also, and shared about deep guilt in her life from an abortion she had many years ago. We prayed through to a real peace in her heart. So the cross marches on touching lives as it goes... I have been hearing from churches across the country who are putting up sign-up boards so folks can pick a day to pray & fast with me the week of July 4-11. Two churches are sending teams to come help for a couple of days. I will be in DC by the end of this June. I have been preaching in 2 different churches a week since I left, sharing the challenge to pray and fast for Revival in this dear country.

Ricks new web site www.rncrosscarrier.org.. A short story as this, is not enough information to let you know the full story. Stay in God's care.

A Mission of Love
Hodge, Jack – TN

He's not a young man, he's not a rich man, but he is a man filled with love for and a desire to help the orphan children of India. He's my brother Robert Hodge 75 years old. Robert was born in Knoxville

Tennessee. Now residing in Pontiac, Illinois. Robert spends a great deal of his time raising money for a mission trip to India each year. Vijaya is an orphan that Robert sponsors. Vijaya's legs are under her, she was born like this and is unable to straighten her legs. In order to get around, she drags her legs under her. Robert stated Vijaya is a very sweet and happy young lady. (If this young girl can be sweet and happy with her infliction, I for one, have nothing to complain about! How about you?) This year will be Robert's fourth trip to the Ongole, India Orphans Home, through the Livingston County Assembly of God Church. These Children are in this home waiting to be adopted, not because they have lost their parents to death but because their parents could not afford to care for them. This orphanage is run by India people with the help of American people. It is a home to 186 children ranging in age from 4 to 18 years old. Roberts mission, to help the children of India. Robert stated "We also buy all the food for the institution while we are there so we are not taking food from the kids. We can buy a lot of rice for a small amount of money and anything we have left from the food fund we create we leave with the orphanage" Robert works with the children, transporting them to and from the Doctor and Dentist for check-ups. This is something that is done for them only in the case of an emergency in normal circumstances. Robert also takes them to activities and talks to them about our Saviour Jesus Christ. You see, if it wasn't for the work of the Missionaries, the children of Orphanage would not be able to do a lot of things we take for granted. Life for those in India is quite different from here at home. We think nothing of turning a knob for water, flipping a switch for light or jumping in the car and going to store. The Villages have no running water or electric. Their water comes from a well, Their living quarters is called a hutch. This is where they sleep and dress. Cooking and everything else is done outside. Robert was telling me one day about the people of India, and how adults and children would run up to him on the street and ask for prayer. If a family is not Christian, and a child accepts Christ they are cast out of the family and considered dead. A seven-day Crusade is held on 10 or 12 acres while Robert is there. Estimated crowd attending is about ten thousand. They sit on the ground for the service. The service starts around 4:30 PM and ends about 11:00

PM or so. Robert stated the alter call takes a long time, as a lot of people come to the alter. Last year the Missionaries raised the funds to purchase several motor bikes. These are used for the workers and ministers to use for their transportation needs for the orphanage. This year the Missionaries will be building a Church. There will be 9 or 10 Missionaries going this year, but before they leave for India they must raise the cost of their fair over, plus living expenses. This is about $2000.00 plus $5,000.00 to build the Church. This is the cost in American dollars. One of our dollars equals forty eight dollars in India. The group raises the money several ways. Things like bake sales, garage sales, odd jobs and donations. Robert was telling me they have to work on the Church in the morning hours. By noon it is very hot and humid. Robert stated "If it gets below 80 the people of India are cold". In the afternoon they will hold youth rallies and visit the Villages where they will witness to the people and the people to them. The men of the Village dance for the Missionaries. My guess, this is their way of saying thank you. The trip to India is a lengthy one. It is an 8 1/2 hour flight from Chicago to London. Then from London to Madras is an 11 hour flight and then from Madras to Ongole is a six hour train trip. "The Indian food is very spicy and almost all of it contains curry. By the time I get back to London the best food in the world seems to be a hamburger." said Robert. Robert said his wife of 52 years fully supports his trips to India but just doesn't care to go along. "I remember everything that happens on each trip so I can tell her when I get home,"

The Gift Of Love
Hodge, Jack – TN

Easter Sunday... What does this day mean to you? You have read of this day many times in the Bible. You have seen the movies Hollywood has made. But have you ever sat down and thought about that day. Put yourself in Jesus place and think having the things done to you that was done to Him. Think about how Jesus was abused and degraded. How the Soldiers stripped Jesus of His clothing and they put on Him a scarlet robe. Jesus was hit over the head with a reed (stalk) and they spit and slapped Him in the face.

Has a thorn of a Rose ever pricked you? Think about a crown of thorns being slammed on your head, I'm sure they were not gentle. How about dragging the very cross on your shoulder you were to be hung on. Jesus was given vinegar and gall to drink when he was thirsty. How about having spikes drove through your hands and feet. Not a pleasant thought. Why would a man go through all this? How much pain and suffering would you endure for one of your children? How much greater is Jesus Love for us than our love is for our children? All the suffering Jesus did for us was because He loves us and wants to save us from a burning Hell for eternity. How can we repay Him for His pain and suffering He did for us? Its easy... Give your life to Jesus, believe Jesus was born of a virgin. Isaiah 7:14 *"Therefore the Lord himself shall give you a sign; Behold, a virgin shall conceive, and bear a son, and shall call his name Immanuel. Butter and honey shall he eat, that he may know to refuse the evil, and choose the good."* Believe Jesus suffered and died on a cross for our sins, in three days rose from the dead. Keep His and our Fathers commandments given to Moses.

As we read the 10 Commandments remember this land was built on the FAITH of our Heavenly Father. Why is the Ten Commandments being removed from so many places? It is clear, fulfilling the scriptures of the Bible. Etch them in your Heart. (The 10 Commandments) Exodus 20 - *I-Thou shalt have no other Gods before me.II-Thou shalt not make unto thee any graven image, III-Thou shalt not take the name of the Lord thy God in vain. V- Honor thy father and thy mother. VI- Thou shalt not kill.*

VII-Thou shalt not commit adultery. VIII-Thou shalt not steal. IX-Thou shalt not bear false witness against thy neighbor. X-Thou shalt not covet thy neighbor's house, thou shalt not covet thy neighbor's wife, nor his manservant, nor his maidservant, nor his ox, nor his ass, nor anything that is thy neighbor's. Take your time and really think about the next passages of scripture I'm giving you. Mathew 9:10-13 *"And it came to pass, as Jesus sat at meat in the house, behold, many publicans and sinners came and sat down with him and his disciples. And when the Pharisees saw it, they said unto his disciples, Why eateth your Master with publicans and sinners? But when Jesus heard that, he said unto them,*

They that be whole need not a physician, but they that are sick. But go ye and learn what that meaneth, I will have mercy, and not sacrifice: for I am not come to call the righteous, but sinners to repentance." What do you get out of the verses? It is our job as a Christian to go out into the world and bring the lost to Christ. Our Churches feed our spiritual needs as a Christian. Our job is to bring the lost out of the world. I have a good friend (Rev. Steve Dawson). Ill bet if you are talking to Steve within 5 minutes of your conversation Steve will be on the subject of Jesus. Not just in Church on the street or any where you may be. "Praise God!" You say you cant talk to people, you don't know what to say.

Many times when I've went to sing some where, I had not a clue what I would say, I was provided with what God wanted said When I started this article, I did not know what I would write. When I write a Poem, I'm given the title to start and the Holy Spirit gives me what to write. I feel blessed as I'm not worthy of the things God has given me to do. I thank my Jesus every day. I pray for Him to lead, guide and direct me in what I say and do. Romans 3:23 *"For all have sinned, and come short of God,"*

A Walking Miracle
Hodge, Jack – TN

Annette Johnson lives in Marion, Ohio. and travels all over the United States singing her praises to God. And why not. Annette is a walking miracle. Let us start at the beginning. Annette came from a Christian home; her Dad was a Minister. At the early age of two Annette would not accept affection from her mother or any one. As Annette stated she was a "mean preachers kid." As Annette grew older she grew worse Annette would sneak out of the house at night to go partying with her friends. Smoking Pot stealing, doing drugs and Drinking. By the age of 16 Annette thought enough was enough of people trying to tell her what she could do and not do. So at a age of sixteen Annette left home, as so many young people do, thinking she could make a better life on her own. Annette wound up living on the slum streets of Chicago. Annette spent three years on the street partying, doing drugs, alcohol, stealing and men. When you get hooked on alcohol and drugs, you will do any thing to get them.

Annette had not had contact with her family in all this time. And her so called friends she was partying with had deserted her. Annette had no one. One day Annette was in an alley and noticed a station wagon coming up the alley. As the wagon got closer she thought her eyes were playing tricks on her, as they often do when you are on drugs and alcohol. It was her Dad, he rolled down the window and said. "I've been looking and praying for you". Annette was scared of what her Dad would say to her. But he said "I Love you and so does Jesus". Annette and her Dad had a long talk. Annette did not go home but got a job in a Christian owned restaurant. Working in this Christian Restaurant was a blessing to Annette. The people would council and have Bible study with Annette. You see Annette was still drinking. Annette did a lot of praying before she could quit drinking. Annette had to get her head and heart together and that took Gods help. Annette said God had never quit dealing with her heart through the years. A quote from Annette. "God has allowed me to be a servant to Him and sing His praises. Telling all who will listen. Its so great to be serving a Miracle working God. Through twenty one cancer-related surgeries, I have found Gods World to be true. He always goes ahead to prepare a way for us. He has never left me alone, even in the darkest hours. When you see me you will see I use a cane, the reason being, my bones are easily broken. I nearly lost the use of my right arm due to cancer surgery in December of 1998 which would have left me in a wheelchair. I'm not complaining, just explaining. God is so Great! He knows my heart and my heart wanted to praise the Lord with both arms lifted up to Him. Through FAITH in God and hard work, I now can lift His praises not only in voice, but with all I have to offer Him. In March 1999, God not only healed my arm but He has also healed my stomach. I was starving to death and went down to "79" pounds. I have recently gained "20" pounds. Praise God! Also in March I was diagnosed with four spots on my liver. The doctor did minor surgery to ease the pain in my rib. During the process they punctured my lung causing it to collapse twice. The doctor told me that I would die if I would try to sing again. I walked out of his office with greater determination to sing for Gods praises and to testify of His goodness. God has opened many doors. "I hope some day to meet you face to face on earth or in heaven, so we can talk and sing the praises forever and ever". I've sang with Annette on several TV shows, and sang in Church services with her. What a joy to hear her testimony and hear her sing. Whatever you are going through, God is waiting to help you. Ask God into your heart. He is the great Physician!

Allah or Jesus?
Mathes, Rick – Location Unknown
I attended my annual training that's required for maintaining my state prison security clearance. During the training session there was a presentation by three (3) speakers representing the Roman Catholic, Protestant, and Muslim FAITHs. These groups explained each of their belief systems.

I was particularly interested in what the Islamic Imam had to say. The Imam gave a great presentation of the basics of Islam complete with a video. After the presentations time was provided for questions and answers.

When it was my turn I directed my question to the Imam and asked "Please correct me if I'm wrong, but I understand that most Imams and clerics of Islam have declared a holy Jihad (Holy War) against the infidels of the world. Islam teaches that by killing an infidel which is a command to all Muslims, they are assured of a place in Heaven. If that's the case can you give me the definition of an infidel?" There was no disagreement with my statements and without hesitation he replied "non-believers!"

I responded, "So, let me make sure I have this straight. All followers of Allah have been commanded to kill everyone who is not of your FAITH so they can go to Heaven. Is that correct?" The expression on his face changed from one of authority and command to that of a little boy who had just gotten caught with his hand in the cookie jar. He sheepishly replied, "Yes!"

I then stated, "Well, sir, I have a real problem trying to imagine Pope John Paul commanding all Catholics to kill those of your FAITH or Dr. Stanley ordering Protestants to do the same in order to go to Heaven! The Imam was speechless.

I continued, "I also have a problem with being your friend when you and your brother clerics are telling your followers to kill me.

Let me ask you a question. Would you rather have your Allah who tells you to kill me in order to go to Heaven or my Jesus who tells me to love you because I am going to Heaven. Jesus wants you to be with me?"

You could have heard a pin drop as the Imam hung his head in shame. Needless to say, the organizers and/or promoters of the "Diversification" training seminar were not happy with my way of dealing with the Islamic Imam and exposing the truth about the Muslim's beliefs.

I think everyone in the U.S. should be required to read this, but with the liberal justice system, liberal media, and the ACLU, there is no way this will be widely Publicized. {**Author's Note**: I don't know Rick Mathes. I've never met or spoken with him. In fact I couldn't find an address or phone number to speak with him before entering his article in this book. I used the last paragraph as permission. I know that a small town paper in Tennessee "Gospel Notes" also published this article. Rick, your article stirred my heart. This book is being published on an International level. Remember – Little is much when God is in it and nothing is too hard for God. God is pleased when we are obedient even if we don't know how he will use it. }

Life's Not Always Easy
Moore, Jim Rev. –TN

God never promised us that life would always be easy, for the Bible says "*Man that is born of a woman is a few days, and full of trouble*" (Job 14:1). This from a man who in just one day, lost all he had. His livestock was stolen, his servants slain, fire from heaven killed his sheep, and a great wind blew his house down upon his children, killing them all. But did Job look to Heaven and curse God, no, but tore his clothes and blessed the name of the Lord. When things do go wrong, you have two choices, curse and turn your back on God, or through FAITH get on your knees and draw nigh to him. Jesus said to his disciples

We will all have to pass through things in this life that, if possible we would choose not to go through. But read the words of James 1:2-4….. "*My brethren, count it all joy when ye fall into divers temptations; Knowing this, that the trying of your FAITH worketh patience. But let patience have her perfect work, that ye may be perfect and entire, wanting nothing"*. It is through the trials and tribulations of this life that we are made strong, that our FAITH is made perfect, and that we become the Christian servant that God would have us to be.

Finally, my friends, I want to share a testimony from my own life with you. Why do I want to do this? For three reasons: #1 – To fulfill a vow that I made to God back in March, 2005; #2 – Because I am not ashamed of the Gospel of Christ, Jesus said "***For whosoever shall be ashamed of me and of my words, of him shall the Son of man be ashamed, when he shall come in his own glory and in his Father's, and of the holy angels***" (Luke 9:26), and #3 – That this testimony that I give will be a help to someone in need....... In the fall of 2003, I became sick. It started off with dizziness and a full-time dull headache. Over the next year and a half, it developed into a bomb in my head. If I coughed, I nearly blacked out; If I sneezed, I nearly blacked out; If I laughed, I nearly blacked out; getting in our out of a car would cause me to almost pass out; if I bent over for any reason, all I seen was stars and blackness; just taking a shower would wipe me out, I would have to lay down for a few minutes before I could do anything else; most of the time, I couldn't even put my own clothes on or tie my own shoes, my wife would have to do it for me. And on tope of all that, I had a constant headache that felt like a jackhammer in my had. I have never been one to take medicine of any kind, but I was eating aspirin or Tylenol like they were candy. In February 2005, I finally gave into to wife and went to our family doctor. He didn't have a clue as to the problem, but the referred me to a neurosurgeon at a local hospital. The neurosurgeon in turn scheduled a series of test on me. On the day of those tests, I spent 3 solid hours in an MRI to check every aspect of my brain, spinal fluids, my cerebral-spinal fluid, and they checked for any fluid leaks. The neurosurgeon scheduled me for another appointment in his office in March.

On that day, he not only told me what the condition was, but he showed me pictures as well. It is a condition where, as a child, my skull never formed correctly, and a small piece of my brain is left exposed at the base of my skull. According to the doc, people that have this condition never know until they enter middle age (I was 45 at the time), then it begins to show up. The problem is, the skull begins to put pressure on the brain, thus the headaches and blackout episodes. He listed every symptom of this condition, and everything that triggered them, and I had every one of them. Now, here was the shocker - he said, I can't touch you, and I can't help you at this time! Why, because even though I had every symptom of this condition, all the tests showed normal, and there was nothing for him to operate on. There were no fluid leaks, fluid levels were good, and the results showed absolutely no pressure on the brain. Why then was I in the shape I was in? Being a completely honest man, he did not know, and best that he could do was to schedule me for another round in August.

Now, here's the whole point of my wanting to share this testimony. When I walked out of the office that day, I knew that one of two things was going to happen…either the good Lord above would heal me, or I would live with and bear this condition the best I could. This is the prayer that I prayed that day… "O Lord, unworthy as I am, I know that you are well able to heal me, You could speak the word only, and I would be healed, if it be thy holy will, But if not, if it be your will Lord that I bear this affliction, then I will bear it to my grave. Your will be done Lord." Isaiah 59:1 says ***"BEHOLD, the Lord's hand is not shortened, that it cannot save; neither his ear heavy, that it cannot hear"***. God heard my prayer that day. He heard the prayers of my family, my church family, and my brothers and sisters in our sister churches who were crying out for me. Praise his holy name, He restored and made me whole! <u>By June, I felt like a new man,</u> able to live life to the fullest once again. By FAITH, I cancelled the re-testing that had been scheduled for August, knowing that God's healing needed no confirmation. The vow I spoke of earlier…. Was a promise to God that if he did see fit to heal me, that I would tell the world about it!

My friends, my story is only one of the many that I know of God's healing grace: My sister has been healed of cancer, my youngest brother spent 9 days in a coma after a car wreck, his brain swelling, and the doctors and all but given up on him, but God hadn't given up and delivered him from his injuries. As a minister, I have a Monday night jail ministry in our county jail. Each week I see God's healing touch upon those broken hearts, broken spirits, and broken lives. He is truly the same God whether you are on the mountain or you are going through a valley. In closing, In leave you these precious words from Matthew 7:7-11: "*Ask, and it shall be given you; seek, and ye shall find; knock, and it shall be opened unto you; For everyone that asketh receiveth; and he that seeketh findeth; and to him that knocketh it shall be opened. Or what man is there of you, whom if his son ask bread, will he give him a stone? Or if he ask a fish, will he give him a serpent? If ye then, being evil, know how to give good gifts unto your children, how much more shall your Father which is Heaven give good things to them that ask him*?" GOD BLESS YOU ALL! {**Author's Note**: FAITH! FAITH! FAITH! It's all about FAITH! I would like to add that Preacher Moore does spend his time now for God. He has a jail ministry that he is very faithful to and passionate about}

God - My Mechanic
Smallwood, Gracie – VA

One Saturday afternoon I went by a little country store managed by my sister and a friend of theirs. My brother-n-law and his friend noticed my car. They came into the store and told me the wheel on the passenger side was about to fall off. I worried all day. I had no one to fix it for me until another payday. My brother-n-law told me to go ahead and drive it about 40 miles per hour and if the wheel did come off it probably wouldn't hurt anything. I remember as I was driving to work that Monday morning and everything on the road was passing me. I began to talk to the Lord. I reminded him of how he had healed me of heart trouble. I told God that many times he had healed me. He had created man and man had made my car, if he could heal me he could heal my car and I'd trust him to do so. All that week I dust drove the car to work and home. On Friday I took it to a service station where whey put it on the rack and checked it out. He told me there was nothing wrong with my car. I asked him if he was sure. He said "Lady 95% of the cars on this road are in worse condition than yours." He didn't even charge me for checking it out. I went straight to the store. My sister was at the store and her friend was a few feet behind her. I announced "God healed my car!" My sister laughed and said Praise the Lord. I thought her friend was going to have a heart attack. Her mouth dropped open and she just looked at me. When she got her composure back she asked me to repeat what I had said. I was more than happy to! "God healed my Car!" I just came from the service station and the man put it on the rack and checked it out. He said there is nothing wrong with your wheels. Thank God, what a mighty God we serve!

Fear Overcome
Smallwood, Gracie – VA

How it started or where I truly do not know, but I was terrified to ride in a car that I was not driving. My greatest fear was of 18 wheelers passing me. This fear caused me to stay home and miss out on a lot of things and places I would have enjoyed.

Our church was having a ladies retreat about 100 miles away. I tried every way to get out of going. I knew the Lord wanted me to go and had met every need fro the trip, except the courage. On Wednesday night prayer service (we were to leave on Friday) I finally told the congregation about my fear. I ask them to anoint and pray for me. I wanted God to deliver me from this fear. He did! Praise the Lord, he did!

We can by God's grace overcome any fear that tries to rule our lives. Many times in the Bible we are told to "fear not" or "be not afraid." Fear of any king (except the fear of God) brings torment to our lives! God wants us to have peace through Christ.

He Feeds the Hungry
Smallwood, Gracie – VA

At this time of my life I was 19 years old. I had three (3) children. We lived in Washington D.C. The apartment we had rented was more than we could pay for, but instead of evicting us he had another apartment on the 1300 block of E. Capital street. My husband had come here to find work but had not. So we moved to the other apartment. The owner let my husband do odd jobs to pay the rent. He also brought us produce that was discounted and ready to get written off, but I found enough good in them to help us eat. Once day my 2 oldest ones said "Mama we are hungry." All I had was a few pieces of spaghetti and a little syrup in the bottom of the bottle. I fixed it let them eat and put them to bed. A neighbor brought over a large box of food that kept us going for a couple of weeks! That had to be Jesus! I had told no one about our need. Out in the garage was a old car. One day my husband got to looking around in the car and found some old dirty coins. He brought them in and we washed them. He took them to the store and got some food. The next time I saw my landlord I told him about what we did. I promised to pay him back as soon I could. He said he did not want it back. The landlord said we could keep any change we found in the car. The car kept us food until my husband found a job and started getting a pay check. God is God, yes he is! He is God all the time!

Hearing the Voice of the Lord
Smallwood, Gracie – VA

This story was told to me by a very dear friend whose gone on to be with the Lord. She was driving her van from Kentucky to Virginia. It was a very mountainous road. She had her arm hanging out window of her car. She heard a still small voice say "You need to get your arm back in the car" She paid it no mind. She kept driving. The message came again saying the same thing. She drove on. The voice came again. This time it was very stern saying "It's needful for you to get your arm back in the car now!" She did and as soon as her arm was in the van she was side-swiped by another car! If her arm had been hanging out the window it would have been torn off. She was so Thankful that she heard and finally listed to God. She was a lot of help t me as I was a growing Christian. I thank God for the friendship we had. One thing she told me I hope I'll never forget she said "I can tell when I'm getting away from God." I ask her how did she know? Her answer was "When I start finding fault in others, I'm not finding fault in me. So I can draw nigh to God for him to forgive me and help me!" I think of this when I start finding fault. Listen for the voice of the Lord. He will guide and protect us. We must listen.

God Is My Provider
Smallwood, Gracie Smallwood –VA

I was living alone in a small apartment. One morning I made a list of several items I needed (food). I layer the list on the table and told the Lord "this is what I need" I wondered how he would provide, but I knew he would. Later that day I net to the post office but no money came in form the mail. I did get a letter from a company that developed my pictures. They told me that they had gotten my order, but no check. That meant my money was still in the bank. Later that day I visited a neighbor. I was showing her a door stop that was an alarm if someone opened the door back on it. She wanted one. It just so happened I had ordered to of them. I only had one (1) door. I sold her the extra. Between the door stop and the un-mailed check I had my needs met. I say that was God's way of providing for me! God works in mysterious ways.

Peace wonderful Peace
Smallwood, Gracie Smallwood –VA

A husband and 7 children is a tough job for any woman. My husband was an alcoholic and ours was a troubled household. On this weekend was especially hard. He had been hard on us all. I was at my end. I did not know what to do. Somehow it past and Monday morning came. With my husband off to work and them children off to school as soon as the door was closed behind them I went to the closest bed and knelt in prayer. My heart was so broken that all I could say was "Oh God". I said it over and over. I don't know how long I stayed on my knees but after a while it felt as if Jesus was sitting on the bed and I had my head in his lap. He just held me. How long I don't know. When I got up from there I felt such a great sense of peace. I went on with my daily work that day. I felt as if I could skip up a mountain side. I sang and worked. The peace of Jesus surpasses all understanding.

Receiving the Holy Ghost
Smallwood, Gracie – VA

I'd like to share and experience I had in April 1977. I had smoked cigarettes for 19 years. I tried many times to quit. Even told the Lord

I'd quit if he'd help me. Now hold on to this thought and I'll get back to it later. My mother took me to a freewill Baptist church until age 10. When we moved to another town. At that time I attended a Pentecostal church for the first time. It sure was different to say the least. We attended that church for about two (2) years. It was the first time I ever heard anyone speak in the Holy Ghost as they did on the day on Pentecost in the book of Acts. I do remember they preached that about everything was a sin. Chewing gum, drinking a coke, cutting your hair, lady's wearing pants, etc. I don't remember much that was not a sin. They sang the song "Time is winding up" Seemed like it went on for and hour or so. I got so tired sometimes I remember wishing it would. I still enjoyed going to church there. We moved back to the old home where my mom took us to the church of God. That was where my mom got the Holy Ghost. I was fascinated by it and scared of the move of the spirit too! I guess I really wanted the Holy Ghost, but I just thought I wasn't good enough. I got married and I moved to another state. Once I left home I never went back to church anywhere for 12 years. The first time I went was for my brother-in-laws funeral. Everyone felt he died lost. He had never been saved. He was working in the coal mines the last thing anyone heard out of him was that he was cursing! It really made me think that if I had been living for the Lord maybe I could have won him for Jesus. After that I started going to a missionary Baptist church in Chicago. That is the way I raised up my children. Then went to the church of the Pentecostal FAITH. My sister's mother-in-law was bedfast and we'd have prayer meetings on Monday night at her house. This was so "ma" could have church. The preacher that held these services had something special in his life that I didn't have. I know that God has no respect of persons. I began to read, study, and pray about this. Up until now I had never ask him for the Holy Ghost. My fear was that if I backslid on the Holy ghost God would never forgive me. On this day before time for church my sister and I went to a restaurant and had a cup of coffee and then went to church. Just before going into the church I put out my cigarette. Sometime during prayer request I ask the people to pray for me that I would get the Holy Ghost. That request shocked me 'cause I had not planned to say that. Through the singing, preaching, etc I didn't think anything more about my request. When the preacher made the alter call he asked me to do the invitation song I got up and walked to the front of the church, but when I got to the alter I told him someone else would have to sing because I had to pray. I don't know how long I prayed but, when I came to myself I realized about everyone had gone home. My sister, the preacher, and me were all that was left. I got up from the alter and I wish I could tell you how I felt. The Bible says "it's better felt than told." I just had to praise the Lord! I could not keep my hands down. I got in the car and very few times my hands held the wheel. Jesus drove my car that night. Most of the time my hands were praising the Lord. After driving about five (5) miles I pulled off the road. The power of God was so strong. I didn't know what to do. It was then that I began to speak in that heavenly language. After a while I don't know how long I drove on to my sister's house about another 2 miles. All the kids I took to church that night except min went home. We sat in the car. My sister, pastor, my children, & I. We just praised the Lord. Finally started home. About another five (5) miles or so. The same thing, heaven came down again. Jesus drove the car. I remember thinking "Lord I have to calm down before I get home! They'll think I'm crazy. I did until my hand touched the door knob and heaven came down and I went in speaking in Holy Ghost. My husband patted me on the back as if to say "you poor thing!" "Poor nothing!" It was the so great I've never been able to tell it. I had to Praise God and am thankful he counted me worthy of his holy spirit in my life. Now back to the cigarettes. Anytime I ever tried to quit I drove my family crazy. I was truly hooked on nicotine. It took me over a week to realize I was not smoking. I don't remember how much longer before my family realized it. I had no withdrawals. It was as if I had never smoked in my life. God wiped it clean out of my life that night. April 2005 has been 28 years. Thank God I have no desire for tobacco in any form. The sweet Holy Ghost is as precious as ever in my life. Praise the Lord!

Trust God
Wynn, Geneva – TN

If I told you everything that God has done for me I could fill a book. He means everything to me. His word promise me health, safety, and prosperity if I put him first in my life.

The first time I can remember him healing me was when I was 18 years old. I had a growth on my eye lid and it became so heavy it was pulling my eye lid down. At that time we had just moved from Virginia to Tennessee. I had no church so I heard Oral Roberts on the radio tell how God could heal. I sent for prayer cloth. I don't even remember when the growth disappeared, but it did! Praise God! He has healed me many more times. I can call the elders of my church and let them anoint me and pray the prayer of FAITH as he says in James 5:14-15. Praise God he heals! **I am almost 67 years old and do not take any medication.**

Sometimes it's hard to turn loose and just trust him. I had a dream once that I was hanging from a very tall tower. My hands were so tired but I was afraid to turn loose. I hung on finally let go. My feet were only inches away from the solid ground. I was too afraid to look down. Sometimes God can't work for us until we let him, but he's always there and ready to catch us.

The most recent devastating thing in my life was about my Grandson. He and his wife had broken up. He took up drugs and drinking. This was bad enough, but then he got involved with a gang. For a long time he was from state to state even went to Canada. The people in this gang were being shot and found dead. By prayer and FAITH God brought him home! During that time our church had called a 24 hour prayer vigil for the lost. I took a picture of him along with my prayer list. I laid them both on the alter. For 24 hours the church prayed for him He was facing lots of problems with the law, but praise God today he's back home with his wife and baby. He has a good job. He hasn't given his live to God yet, but by FAITH and prayer he will be saved! Praise God for prayers are answered. {**Author's Note:** Geneva is very knowledgeable in the scriptures and a great prayer warrior}

Electricity
Name Withheld – TN

My husband and I hadn't been married too long. I was pregnant with our only child. I was only working part time and we had just moved into a new apartment. The apartment complex gave us two (2) weeks to switch the electricity to our name. I called the electric company to do this. She told me that we would require a deposit of $100. I know $100 doesn't sound like much, but it is a lot if you don't have it. I was to proud to ask for help, and my family didn't have the money anyway. I wasn't even living right, but I got down and prayed. "Jesus, please make a way, please see me through this, please" I prayed and prayed. I called the electric company back. The girl found an exception and we did not have to pay that deposit. They transferred our electric service! God made a way for us even though I wasn't living right and my husband wasn't even saved.

A Prayer in The Darkness
Name Withheld - TN

I was awoken suddenly from a good sleep. A friend of ours was on my heart. I thought this was especially strange because I hadn't seen or talked with this person in a while. I thought to myself "God does work in mysterious ways." I was wide awake and it was the middle of the night. I felt an urgency to pray for this friend. I was so scared for this friend. I prayed and prayed still not understanding why. The next day I learned that during that night my friend had been in a car accident! The friend was unharmed. Glory to God! I am so thankful he uses me as unworthy as I am. Thank you Jesus!

CHAPTER 4

<u>FAITHFULLY WRITTEN</u>

(**Hebrews 11:3** *Through FAITH we understand that the worlds were framed by the word of God, so that things which are seen were not made ofthings which do appear.)*

Lets Be Open-Minded?
Yong Cong - Singapore

It disturbs me to see that.. while we're pushing ourselves to be more open-minded, more receptive, we're tolerating ideas and societal behavior that clashes against the very fabric of what we believe in, and at the same time, compromising on our own values system, thus, losing our own individuality, becoming fake, and giving in to external pressure under the facade of "lets be more matured about this."

Yah rite. indiscriminating open-mindedness is not bringing our society forward. it is tearing the very fabric which it is sewn upon. We must still have the courage to say NO, we don't want this in our society. There must be a limit to this.. open-mindedness. C'mon. give a thought to it. Some things are JUST wrong and not worthy of acceptance. {**Author's Note**: Ok – Christians want to hear something interesting about Yong? He doesn't believe in Jesus. I asked

Yong this question "Do you believe in Jesus Christ and salvation?" Yong's answer: "I'm a freethinker and no, I don't believe in Christ even though I have a bunch of close friends who do. Ultimately, nothing has convinced me of the FAITH just yet." I'll let you make your own conclusions, but I think Yong obviously has an excellent moral and value system. I wish more Christians would proclaim that some things are "JUST wrong" the way that Yong has. I pray that someday Yong will be convinced of the FAITH. God has to draw people, but the light we let shine helps lead them to Christ. People like Yong will have a really hard time finding there FAITH if they never see us the born again body of believers taking a stand. Yong, when you read this – I thank you from the bottom of my heart and pray God's blessing upon you.}

Wind Bubbles
Dyer, Amy – TN

I was outside with my child one day. We were enjoying the beautiful weather. I was blowing bubbles for him. He loves playing with bubbles. The wind was blowing and I noticed the bubbles were blowing in the same direction of the wind. The same speed and everything. I know this seems simple but, all at once the spirit of the Lord spoke to my heart. I thought of that verse in St. John 3:8 *"The wind bloweth were it listeth, and thou hearest the sound thereof, but cans't not tell whence it cometh, and whether it goeth: so is every one that is born of the Spirit."*

You may not be able to see the spirit of God in physical form, but you can feel him. The wind is the same way. You can't see it, but you can't deny that it is there. You see the evidence of the wind in the trees, grass, our hair, etc. The Spirit of God like the wind at times can give you chill bumps. {Author's Note: I really enjoyed this entry. We often times try to make FAITH complicated.. Our walk with the Lord is as simple as bubbles in the wind. We walk with God through FAITH. FAITH is not complicated. Amy, I pray God blesses you for this illustration that makes it clear and easy to understand.}

Fishing Preacher
Dyer, Jason -TN

(Child of God) I know the Lord wants me to be a fisherman, but I think I'm using the wrong bait. (Preacher) Are you using the word of God as bait? (Child of God)Yes. (Preacher) Maybe you aren't living the bait out long enough.

A Star Was Born
Hodge, Jack - TN

A star was born on Christmas day, I have something you can't take away, Deep within this heart of mine, Jesus, a spirit, so true and kind. Yes, it's the star of Bethlehem, I know he's real, I can feel him, He rules my life day and night, I keep him close and never loose sight. Yes, my star is true and strong, Given his word it can't be wrong. Won't you accept my star today? All it takes is to kneel and pray. You'll have a spirit living within, Guiding you through a world of sin. Yes, this star that's strong and true, He'll never leave or forsake you. Jesus is the star I'm talking about, he lives in my heart I have no doubt. And he is coming back to take me home., On this earth, I will no more roam. Oh yes, the star of Bethlehem, My Lord, My Saviour, I can depend. He walks by my side night and day, so you see, I'm going his way. {**Author's Note**: This was written by-Jack Hodge 3:AM November 25 , 2000 (c) Published By Noble House of London, Paris & New York , International Library Of Poetry, American Poets and Famous Poets Society}

A Fresh New Day
Hodge, Jack – TN (Written July 29, 2001)

As the rain gently falls; a gentle breeze whispers free. Starts out a fresh new day God has made for you and me. The air smells clean and it is beginning to get light. Oh what a feeling inside and all seems so right. With this new day we have been blessed to receive We can make it a joy and something new we can receive. If we open our hearts and take what God has to give. Enjoy all His beauty and love and a new day to live. We have been so blessed as I think of days of old. Working from dawn to dusk back-breaking work I've been told. God keeps giving us tools to rest. My, My, how we've been blessed. With this new day we've given, a lot of FAITH and trust. To tell someone along the way. His love, its here to stay.

A Misty Day
Hodge, Jack – TN (Written September 20, 2001)

The rain is gently falling. It's running down my face. I thank God for the mountains and His loving grace. He placed me in the mountains. Away from the big city life. There I'll never return again. I wont have to think twice. There the pace is much too fast. It is hard to catch your breath. Caught up in a world of stress but now Ill try and do my best. As I look across the way, a word of kindness in prayer I do say. For all the wealth He has given to me. A family in my heart forever to be. In the distance the mist I see. God made the beauty for you and me. The bear, the fawn scampering around. And the birds in the trees. Ah, such beauty all around. Away from the big city can be found. So take a walk on a misty day. As you walk you can pray.

A New Life
Hodge, Jack – TN (Written March 29, 2001)

We have a chance for a new life. We must never look back or think twice. The way to salvation is clearly marked. All it takes is for us to do our part. A man called Jesus, he hung on a cross. To save us from a life that was wicked and lost. The Father above was sorry he made us. Jesus spoke up and said, "Father give me your trust". So to this earth He came to save us from hell. Why do some shy away from Christ and rebel? Follow his lead and to others you must tell of a place called Heaven where we can dwell. Now this man called Satan has lost the fight. He knows he is wrong and never been right. He had his chance once in Heaven above. His greed destroyed Gods precious love. Gods mighty arm is on the move. All over the world they're out to prove. Jesus was here, He is well and alive. He will be back, with Him we will abide. The spirit tells me what to say and do. What you do with it, it is up to you. So take this history, lock it in your mind. A plan so simple, you wont be left behind.

A Talk With Jesus
Hodge, Jack – TN (Written June 30, 2001)
I have been asked to go far away. With my music for me to play. To sing of the coming of our Lord. To bring the message of His great reward. Yes, to India I've been asked to go. They are hungry for Jesus I was told. The young and the old ask you to pray. When its time to leave, you are begged to stay. It is so sad the stories I've been told of there. My heart is so heavy; its time to be aware. Has the love for our brothers as we are told Taking Jesus word everywhere, yes we must go. Jesus will soon be coming it is close at hand. So we must go wherever across this land. Letting all see the love of Jesus inside. And forever with him you want to abide. Yes, I said I would go wherever I was sent. To do Your work, the time will be well spent. So Ill ask these things Jesus of you. Lead and guide me in all I say an do.

Birthday – December 25
Hodge, Jack – TN (Written December 06, 2005)
With the eyes of Jesus looking ahead Seeing our works and His word did we spread. Keeping a book with many names inside Will He find yours or will you be left behind? Our time is short in this land we know Following Jesus, that is the way to go!
When the book is opened, your name called out, Your feet will dance, your mouth will shout. All your treasures in heaven are safely stored. But to see Jesus will be the greatest reward. So this Christmas remember what this day is for. Our Christ and Saviour was born in days of yore.

Flight of The Dove
Hodge, Jack - TN (Written November 10, 2001)
As the dove flies across the skies, spreading his wings; oh my, my! The peaceful feeling I get inside. My Saviour, Jesus, for me He died. To save my soul from a burning hell. Now in Heaven with Him I will dwell. To see the love ones that went on home. On this earth I will no more roam. I cant explain the feeling I get inside. What He did for me. I fill with pride. To think of the years I wasted in sin. Cheating my Saviour and where I've been. As the dove sits

his wings in flight. Spreading out wide, oh what a site! As he flies across the sky so blue. In perfect balance, strong and true. A snow white dove, a flight in host. A reminding symbol of the Holy Ghost. Watching His flock. Soaring across the sky. Until it is time to this world to say goodbye.

He is My Greatest Pride
Hodge, Jack – TN (Written June 11, 2001)

As I ponder over my life I feel how fortunate to have God by my side. as to the things I've done in my past. He has forgiven. His love will last. As we talk and plan out my life Ill go forward and never think twice. To do Gods work as He would have me to; to Him be FAITHful and true. He is with me night and day. From His side I will never stray.

From Him comes wisdom you see. Walking with Him is where I want to be. Yes, the courage He gives me to go on. He is always there to make me strong. He is the light that fills my soul. He is the greatest story ever been told. I never tire of writing of Him. So I'll keep on writing, this is my whim. Ill keep doing the best I can. You know He will make me a better man. Sometimes the excitement I feel inside rushes through me like the tide. You can see He is my greatest pride. So with Him I will forever abide.

My Father
Hodge, Jack – TN (Written June 01, 2001)

My father is rich. He's a King on His throne. He is always with me. I'm never alone. His word is sufficient. It's true and strong Listen to my Father, He is never wrong. He will lead and guide you In all that you say and do. All you have to do is ask Him. He will keep you from being lonely and blue. He's given us a choice of Heaven or Hell.Just keep His commandments; with Him we will dwell. We must be cautious not to be led astray. Yes, our Father, we must obey. As I read the words of my Father above. He has taught me to have brotherly love. To always lend a helping hand. To someone close or across the land. Yes, my Father is rich. He's the owner of it all. Ill claim what is mine while walking tall. Yes, when He comes to take us away. There in His Kingdom forever I'll stay.

My Task
Hodge, Jack – TN (Written July 4, 2001)

What a blessing on me has been bestowed. To think our Lord Jesus, me he has chosen; to spread His returning around the world. As I think of my task, sets me in a whirl! I must choose carefully as to what I say and do. People are watching. Jesus will see me through. I know it is time for our Saviour to return. Now more than ever its time we learn. If we don't repent to Hell we will go. There we will burn forever, we've been told! Now let me tell you about living for Christ. I've found out, that it is quite nice. You can have fun with family and friends. Talking and laughing, that's not a sin. Being a Christian it is wonderful to me. Not like some things. Its great to be set free. The Devil would have you think its a bore. But the Devil messed up in days of yore. He thought he could take the place of God. Now in Hell forever the Devil must trod. Let the Holy Spirit take you on a high. There is nothing like it, again you'll want to try. To get that feeling with eagles you will soar. Yes, you'll want to stay, you'll beg for more. I have this feeling of happiness, yet sad. For those that are lost, I feel so bad.

It doesn't take much to be saved from Hell. To go to Heaven and there forever dwell. Just ask Jesus to forgive your sins and never return back to Satan's Den. You will be living a life that is great. Your heart filled with love and not with hate. Oh this feeling of happiness I have inside. Knowing with Jesus forever I will abide. To see friends and family that went on before. There are no sick, old, lonely, black, white or poor. Now is the time, stand or kneel and pray. You will be forgiven of your sins today. You will have this feeling I have deep within. And Jesus will wipe away your life of sin.

Our Debt
Hodge, Jack – TN (Written August 2001)

The time is coming, I'm truly blessed. I'm on my way to a haven of rest. He leads me down the roads I must trod. Laying the foundation by laying the sod. Watering everyday to make the roots strong. I know our Lord is coming, it wont be long. He gives me the words to others I must say. I hope you listen to Jesus, this I pray. You have the power, my brother, forever to live. With Jesus in Heaven, He freely gives. He paid a price on Golgotha long years past. When He hung on a cross, gave a love to last. Let us pay our debt with a love for the King. By keeping His word forever true and clean.

Prayer of FAITH
Hodge, Jack – TN (Written June 21, 2001)

As I prepare for the work you have in store and this trip to old friends and days of yore. Give me the words to set them free from sin And never to return back to satin's den.The life we led in our days of youth. May my friends see in me words of truth. Of the things you have changed in my life. I'm going forward; Ill never think twice. So I'll stand on this Prayer of FAITH. Doing your work, to enter Heavens Gates. Someone's life may be touched and set free. God this is what I ask of you from me.

Standing on the Rock
Hodge, Jack – TN (Written 2001)

Standing on the Rock where living waters flow. Standing on Gods word wherever I may go. His word is sufficient. On Him I can depend. Through the trials of life, never to return to where I've been. He leads me over the mountains, through the Valley of Yore. He talks to me daily and with eagles I will soar. Oh His living water that floods my soul. I know the greatest story that has ever been told. So Ill keep on standing on the solid rock and Ill live forever in the presence of His flock.

Stress Nine One-One
Hodge, Jack – TN (Written September 20, 2001)

As the days pass by and the smoke clears the sky, my heart is filled with sorrow for those lost, I cry. For those left behind an awakening there should be. Such an evil happening, it could have been you or me. Now as we face tomorrow much heartache and pain. All the loving mother's, it puts an awful strain. Ah, but a greater force can take us through all this. Just call out his name. With Jesus there's no risk. There was another day even more cloudy that last. That day was called Calvary, a day long past. Jesus hung on a cross to save us from a place called Hell. If we follow His will, some day in Heaven we will dwell. The warning signs are here. They flood my mind. So give your heart to Jesus. Don't get left behind.

Thanksgiving
Hodge, Jack – TN (Written November 20, 2003)

On a winters crisp November morning and the leaves are falling to the ground. The fog hovers over the meadow. The sounds of wildlife all around. A gentle breeze blows across my face. an early morning mist I do embrace. The day of Thanksgiving is at hand. We are blessed to live in this land. The aroma of roasted turkey fills the air. All pies have been baked, set out in pairs. Stuffing with chestnuts, cranberry sauce, candied yams, peas and salad tossed. We'll be blessed with family and friends. A big, big spread, yes that's the trend. When dinner is over were all stretched out. Me in my chair and maw on the couch. Ill bless this day in a land to be free. Thank the men fighting for you and me. Praying soon they'll all be home to stay. Never forgetting God gave us this day.

The American Soldier
Hodge, Jack – TN (Written October 20, 2005)

The American Soldier in time of war. Is put through hell, but with Eagles He Soars. To protect our country from men of woe. Away to a foreign country, they must go. Our life is held in their brave - brave hands. Fighting for us, they have taken a stand. It is up to us to cheer them on. Praying to God to bring them home. Making their way through this foreign land. Pushing on, through the heat, rain, dust and sand. In a country filled with men of hate, lust and greed. It will take God, in their hearts to plant the seed. As I sit here safe and secure in my home. I'm sure you are frightened and feel alone. God is your friend, reach out and take His hand. He will keep you safe and secure in this foreign land. {Adopted by Operation Military Parents as their Theme Poem}

The Angel
Hodge, Jack – TN (Written December 31, 2001)

What color is an angel? What do you see? Are we not all the same? No color nor creed? Instead of our eyes we should look with our hearts. We all were the same from the very start. When we are in Heaven no colors there. Well be all the same, no eyes will compare. Our brothers and sisters will all be the same. There will be no calling of cynical names. The day is coming, well join hand in hand. When we reach heaven all will be grand. All there will be loved and treated as one. No color well see, And all will have won.

The Armor
Hodge, Jack – TN (Written September 20, 2001)

As I grow older and think back through the past, Some time that was wasted, other things I know will last. Some mistakes I have made, other days Id never trade. Fond memories that last forever, others a price was paid. There is a day foretold of all the past we will not remember. Strength and peace comes from the One born in December. We must put on the armor to face the evils of today. That means getting on your knees and to our Father pray. We knew this day was coming. It is written in the Book. We must focus on the scriptures. We must take another look. There is a greater power. He keeps pressing on my mind. I know Him as my Jesus. He has made Heaven mine.

The Holy Spirit
Hodge, Jack – TN (Written August 05, 2001)

The Holy Spirit stays in my mind. Giving me words so you wont be left behind. The short time we have to spend on earth. Read my words of truth and of His worth. The warning signs, they are everywhere. Now it is time we must be aware. Accept the voice that speaks within. Its time to leave this world of sin.

The Journey
Hodge, Jack – TN (Written January 31, 2002)

As I travel through this life here to and fro, there is so much I don't understand or know. I press on with the work you have for me in store. Just knowing one day with you I will soar. Oh the beauties that fills my mind of days ahead. The journey with you on water I may tread. There are those I'm sure who don't understand. What you and I have, I think its grand. To be a part of the work to save some soul and working in the greatest story ever told. Sometimes I fill with such love and grace. From where I've been and now in this place. There's no other place Id rather be, I'm free. Thinking of what lies ahead for you and me when I walk through those Gates of Gold. Thank you Jesus for saving my wicked soul!

The Shadow of My Lord
Hodge, Jack – TN (Written May 29, 2001)
    Walking in the shadow of my Lord I am greatly blessed and Heaven is my reward. Keeping His word and spreading His news of His returning to get me and you. He will take us to a home beyond the sky. Well live there forever, if only we will try to obey His Commandments. (The Golden Rules) Give all we have and to Christ be true. Oh, the joy that fills my soul knowing there well never grow old. No more sickness, no more pain. We've nothing to lose and everything to gain. On the throne my Jesus does reign. The devil has lost; he's in a strain. Trying his best to overcome his downfall.He is finished. He can never return over that wall. Oh yes, he knows he cant win. He went on his own and chose a life of sin. Now he tries his best to pull us into his den. Painting a great picture of beauty as he pretends. Oh yes, he is cunning and his words are smooth. He will show you great beauty he will give to you. He knows your weakness and there he will start But to him reply, "I apply the blood, from me depart!" So I'll keep walking this road of my King. To me I know I'll receive everything He promised to me. Heaven is my reward so I'll keep walking in the shadow of my Lord.

The Spirit Spoke
Hodge, Jack – TN (Written July 04, 2004)
    The Holy Spirit woke me around three. Said "write these words I give to thee". "A Star Was Born", was what I was given. Nothing more, I lay there with misgivings. I said to the Spirit, "I have nothing

to write". It was very late, wee hours of the night. The Spirit said "get up, there is work to do". when I got up I found out this was true. As I typed the words began to flow. It was telling a story of long, long ago. Our Lord and Saviour, Jesus Christ; I have found Him to be my greatest vise. When I had finished the poem given me, The Spirit spoke again these words to me. "You must write a book to help others along; to give them strength, FAITH and to be strong". As we fight against Satan and his crew; the words in my book I know will help you. This book will tell you there is coming a day. Our Lord Jesus will be back to take us away. Now the Spirit is giving me poems everyday. To get these poems published is what I pray. But with patience Ill be shown what to do. As the Spirit will lead me. I know this is true.

Trust
Hodge, Jack – TN (Written June 10, 2001)
There are those with their smile so sweet and you are blessed when you first meet. You may feel their true and most kind. But I've found, beware, do not be blind. Don't be fooled by their cunning ways. What you felt was true. It starts to fade. Then comes the hurt you feel deep within. If you deceive your brother is it not a sin? Oh the trust and FAITH that we put in man as we try getting along doing the best we can. To be a friend, kind, loving, FAITHful and true but to turn your cheek the Bible says you must do. Yes there is one on whom we can depend. His name is Jesus. What a true friend. He will never forsake or leave your side. In Christ you will forever and ever abide.

Volcano
Hodge, Jack – TN (Written May 04, 2005)
The volcano that is deep inside the earth. The hot burning ashes giving out a burp. Lava bubbles running a stream of hot ash. Rumbling and swelling, spreading like a rash. As you look deep inside this red hot den. Look over your life. See where you have been. Could this deep, deep hole possibly be hell? This is a place you would not want to dwell. Escape this furnace that will burn to eternity. turn to the one that holds peace and serenity. You must confess your sins from

the heart. Cling to Jesus, from His word never depart. You have turned from that hole called hell. Keep walking on, to the past say farewell. All the peace and joy in Jesus you will find. Keep looking forward. Never looking behind.

Well Done My Child
Hodge, Jack – TN

As I watch and listen to my fellow Christians each day I ask myself and wonder if they're headed the right way. The jealousy and greed from our brothers of love. Sometimes Id like to fly away on the wings of a dove. There is much talk; putting down one church to another is wrong. I'm sure because of all this my Jesus is smothered. Looking down to see what He came here to die for. All that He did for us; is He not due much more? Step back and take a look at all you do and say. The hurt you may cause your brother, a price you may pay. As you stand before our God on that Judgment Day
He will say "well done my child", this I pray.

What a Beautiful Day
Hodge, Jack – TN (Written June 21, 2000)

The sun is shining. The grass is green. The mountains are a bluish gray. Oh what a beautiful day. Talking with Jesus as I stray. I'm dreaming of heaven and our Host. Feeling the Spirit of the Holy Ghost. I know my God is here to stay. He gives me great peace when I pray. Oh yes what a beautiful day! As I walk across this field of bliss I'm counting my blessings with a jest. So you see I'm happy to say, Thank God! What a beautiful day. There is much more to sing about I know this in my heart. I have no doubt. So why don't you stroll this way! Oh yes; what a beautiful day!

White Puffs Against The Blue
Hodge, Jack – TN (Written August 17, 2001)

The white clouds nestled in the sky. Looks like puffs of cotton. On them we could fly. Take a trip to a place beyond the blue. Spreading love everywhere straight and true. So take my hand, to dreamland we will go. All my love on you I will bestow. Your are the one beyond my wildest dreams. Together, forever, we will make a team. The beauty you will see along the way will stick in your mind, its there to stay. All that God has given to us. Placed in our hands with His trust. We must take care and not destroy what He has given to share and much more. All the beauty on Earth and in the sky is ours to enjoy; given from our father on high. As the sun sinks in the west I hope to all I've given my best.

Words From The Spirit
Hodge, Jack – TN (Written October 17, 2001)

The power of the Holy Spirit filled my mind today. The Spirit is telling us we need to kneel and pray. For this world as we know it is coming to a close. As the Book is fulfilled from the day Jesus arose. The time is drawing near for Jesus to return. If you are not ready in hell you will surely burn. what an awful thought to think, "forever burn". Living for Him is easy while waiting for His return. He gave us Ten Commandments to follow each day. These Commandments are very easy if daily we pray. Our Saviour is there to help us in all we say and do. His word is sufficient and we know His love is true. We have been forewarned, the word is very clear. Our God is very jealous; it is He we must hold dear. Put Satan behind you. Satan's battle was always lost. Jesus has the victory and Him you don't want to cross. I'm looking forward to Heaven. A mansion built for me. Walking down those streets of gold and my Jesus to see. Now I'm getting excited. I'm getting all warm inside. There we will live forever. We will never again say goodbye. As I put these words on paper given by the Spirit inside. Never knowing what the end will be; I take great pride! To have the Spirit pick me to deliver a message to you. About the word of Jesus and I know these words are true.

World Peace
Hodge, Jack – TN (Written January 22, 2002)

World peace would be an easy task if to our Father above we would ask For brotherly love to fill our hearts, down on our knees is the place to start. Ah, there is so much we all have on our table! It started long ago with Cain and Able. The greed that fills the hearts of each man, before its too late, we must take a stand. To bring together a world filled with peace. With brotherly love to all we must reach.

A kind word, a helping hand to those in need. Most of all to wipe away lust, hate and greed. Just like in war an army is needed here. Spreading through this world love and cheer. The blood that was shed on the cross long ago won the battle so to Heaven we could all go. Now I am but a humble man with a plan. With simple words I give wherever I can. To show a life that fulfills and soothes within and maybe help rid the world of war and sin.

Sin
Pelfrey, Charlene –TN

You can't go down a chimney without getting a little suet on you! {Author's note – Lot's of times people justify the things they do by saying "I was there, but I didn't participate". Sin is Sin.} Author's Note: This is my Mama and growing up I heard this more times than I can count. I never really appreciated it until I began trying to live for God.

The Battle of Winter
Sheppard, Jerry -TN

I pray we don't meet in a battle of winter, Instead I pray it is the life of spring better the heat of summer. But if it is in the battle of winter my camp I will not share warmth and food you'll find not there. And if you call me friend I'll be forever foe For if we meet in a battle of winter Your body a guest will the Earth hold. It is better I say we meet in the battle of summer and that the heat of love will hold 'til winter not be seen.

In the beginning – Alpha & Omega
Sheppard, Jerry - TN

In the beginning God created the heaven and earth. Genesis 1:1

A common problem exists whether one is contemplating any religion, other than that of the Jewish and Christian FAITH, or the concept of Science, so called (science does not extend far enough) as also the religions of re-incarnation, The failure of science is that of common definition gone amok or astray, either make the definition correct or call the hypothesis what it is – a cruel joke on scientist who have accepted ignorance instead of fact. The fact: The scientist have long concluded that at one time there was a void – a nothing – then they state in direct contradiction to all they have been taught, something appeared out of nothing (thus the definition has become invalid). Atoms are the basic building block of all matter and that being the case of the Big Bang what properties were the two atoms composed of hydrogen, wood, glass, etc.. And what or who pushed these two atoms into each other? Mankind used to think in depth and question this type of fraudulent claims, but now they are readily accepted by the populace. If there is truth in "nothing" then these two Atoms of a necessity had to have been introduced by another source, which leaves only creation as a source or we must violate the word "nothing". Atheists have long been the thinkers of society since they (except in recent time) had nothing to prove but facts themselves (consider C.S. Lewis atheist to Christian). Buddhist, Hindu, and other re-incarnationsists fail at the onset as they preclude to continue in re-incarnation until ascension to a plane called "Nirvana" which means "nothing" which has been shown as non-existence. One oddity here should be stated as that of Cain who slew his brother: ***"And Cain went out from the presence of the Lord, and dwelt in the land of Nod, on the east of Eden"*** Gen 4:16. The word "Nod" is stated to be defined as "nothing" this could be what generations have termed as "Nirvana" and became such as religion.

Buddhist claim dissension (as do) Hindu, who worship many Gods) from Buddha Hich came from Buddha, etc... (To the nth degree), however, Buddha's beginning was the son of a king who had five maids to attend to him. His name? Guatemala Siddhartha who introduced that the problem with man was his desire for materialism, thereby, minus the desire for things and the problem would be solved. So Siddhartha concluded, if the people gave all their possessions to the King, the King could give back what the needed instead of their wants. We used to call this system the "Commune System" another derivative of the word communists". Who then would be the benefactor of this system? Siddhartha's dad, the king and ultimately Siddhartha's himself – not bad for a thinker, huh? So how then is truth expressed to what or to whom can we attribute truth?

Truth must remain consistent – a popular statement among those who oppose absolute truth declare truth as "relative" truth as though truth is dependent upon circumstances or relative to the situation you find yourself in, if, that were the case then relative truth fails because it is not an absolute. Truth that changes becomes fake, fraud, or a lie at some point. So where can we explain where God comes from? The big question! It is found in a few versed located in the book of James - New Testament – King James Version Bible. *"Let no man say when he is tempted, I am tempted of God: for God cannot be tempted with evil, neither tempteh he any man: But every man is tempted, when he is drawn away of his own lust, and enticed. Then when lust have conceived, it bringeth forth sin: and sin, when it is finished, bringeth forth death."* James 1: 13-15. {**Author's Note**: This was written by a very intelligent man who wrote this on a higher level than the majority of us myself included, read regularly. I believe the premise behind his writing is direct and simple. God is, was, and has always been. Religion and/or denomination are not important as much as FAITH through grace by Jesus Christ. Those of us with the FAITH know science is incorrect because we believe each and every word printed in God's Holy word, the Bible. If you are interested in more of Mr. Sheppard's literature visit spantalk@ blogspot.com}

The Damned/A People Soon Acquainted With Death
Sheppard, Jerry – TN

"He that hath ears to hear, let him hear. But whereunto shall I liken this generation? It is like unto children sitting in the markets, and calling unto their fellows, And saying, We have piped unto you, and ye have not danced; we have mourned unto you, and ye have not lamented." - Matthew 11:15-18

The Late Great Planet Earth The Rapture Left Behind The Prophecy The Passion The Chronicles of Narnia/The Lion, The Witch and The Wardrobe The Lord of The Rings 7th Heaven The Ten Commandments The Greatest Story Ever Told The Gospel of John all movie or television productions ....Disasters: Hugo, Andrew, Katrina, 911, At the moment of impact the people reacted to the point of filling the churches during 911 but later cursing these same churches and their drive to keep society clear of the evil which is now and soon to come.

A reminder of such are those associated with public needs such as education - The Lottery - Gambling, Sacrificing of children for the sins of the parent - abortion, The soon developing law of legal sex with children - United Nations "Rights of the Child" which redefines the age of a child to have the rights of an adult, this allowing adults to have sex with children, introduction of sexual activity such as Lesbianism, Homosexuality, now running rampant in schools- elementary as well as high schools-introduced by a President of the United States.

Now if any of this makes you angry ask yourself why, after all they are no more than words on pages, but the anger stems from something inside you which states you are headed for judgment, the time is set and the judgment sure. Note this generation which GOD speaks highly of their attitudes and reasoning.

You must bear in mind he is called the "anti-Christ" who opposes all that God has blessed and seeks to destroy any resemblance to that which is of God. The things God instituted and that which the serpent opposes: Marriage -soon to be against the law for a male and female but ordained for partners of same sex. Common laws such as speeding, murder, rape, theft and other such illegal activity will be condoned and actually rewarded; child molesters get less time now than those who kill an animal or steal, theft was shown in L.A. and those areas of disasters have to be policed to stop looters, rape is viewed as minor crime even by women's groups if they are in oppo sition to the victim, etc..... Eating of flesh as mentioned above will once again be encouraged as it was in Rome when Jesus walked the earth, because of hunger and malnourishment men/women will eat their own children and some will devour their own arms and flesh. Because food will be produced in a laboratory instead of the fields of the earth it will have little to no value to the body. Ask yourself has this occurred in your day? Will it not occur soon, even when the church is removed?

Dear Jesus
Sheppard, Teresa – TN

Dear Jesus, Oh it's gorgeous! Thank you, for bringing me here. I bet my mommy is saying "How beautiful Heaven must be". I am sure you told her that you came for me. I know she must miss me terribly, but glad all the same because you are here to hold me.

The last thing I remember is being grabbed away from her. I tried to get close to Mommy, but my murderer persisted until my life was gone. My pain didn't last long because of you, oh Lord dear Jesus. Thank you for coming to my rescue!

I hate to ask you for another favor you've already been so good to me. What with giving me this beautiful mansion on high and all the angels to sing me to sleep, but my good and FAITHful father, if you would please when my mommy's life is over…bring her to me. It would make everything complete. For my murderer, please send them a message so they will know that what they put me through, and let them know about all the marvelous things you had in store for my earthly life. I will surely be missed. Again, Thank you Jesus! Signed, Aborted Baby. Gen.33:5: "*And he lifted up his eyes, and saw the women and the children; and said Who are these with thee? And he said, The children which God hath graciously given the servant.*"

My Grapes
Sheppard, Teresa Sheppard - TN

She saw the frantic look on his face as he walked down the dead end street in his neighborhood. "Sir, can I help you find something or someone?" Have you seen my grapes? I haven't seen any grapes on my vine! Have you ever seen my grapes? Tell me if you have! I must have grapes; I surely must have some, somewhere! "What are you talking about? You don't own a grape vine." No, not the kind you eat. The Bible says Jesus is the vine, we are the branch, I don't understand why I am not bearing spiritual fruit. A Christian would have at least 2 or 3 grapes on their branch. "How did you become the branch?" I joined a church and I pay my tithes. What more can I do? "Were you saved by God's grace?" I am not sure exactly, but I must be. The minister told me I was saved. I haven't missed a service and I never skip out on my tithes. "Salvation has nothing to do with church membership or your tithes. Those are both good things, but they will not take you to Heaven." How exactly is it I am supposed to get to Heaven? I've been reading about Heaven and Jesus. I really believe. I want to go to Heaven and I don't want anybody to go to Hell! I believe Hell is as real as Heaven. I just don't understand this whole religion thing or how it works. Why doesn't God send me an answer? "Here is the name and address of a church, you come Sunday to hear the preached word and you'll begin to understand." I may not have time for that. I might die tonight! "Let's pray together right now." He began to pray: Jesus I believe you are real, I don't understand religion, but I understand Heaven and Hell. Pleas save me from Hell.

With a loud AMEN he knew he was saved. He began to jump up and down screaming and shouting while running down the street. Yes indeed, it was there on that street he received his salvation, because Jesus was calling him. He was so high in the spirit he forgot about the neighbor he'd been talking with. He knocked on every door looking for her. He wanted to thank her for praying with him and to tell her he got saved! He never found her. He did find the Bible preaching church she told him about. Not one person at the church knew who she was. He became so involved in his work for God he forgot about her. A kind stranger yes, but his salvation came from the Lord Jesus. He began to understand the Christian way. He became a good solider for God. Before long, he saw his grapes. A few here or there. He told his wife he was happy to know he did have a few grapes for the Lord.

Years went by; the man died and went to Heaven. He faced judgment. Jesus said: "My good and FAITHful servant enter in…. and my child about the grapes, you not only produced a few for me, but through you obedience to me the seeds you planted are enough for a vineyard! About the kind stranger lady who prayed with you, (in an instant she appeared), She said "I am an angel of the Lord; he sent me to you that day to help you find your answer! Welcome home my brother!

ShutUp!
Teresa Sheppard - TN

I was thinking these thoughts during a recent church service: Is he ever going to shut up? I really wish he would shut up! Doe he think there are people here who haven't heard his testimony? Ok, so he got saved, good for him, we all know, so he can shut up! Doe he believe that anyone in this church cares about what he is saying. Shut up already.

The person sitting beside me was thinking these thoughts: Is he ever going to shut up? I really wish he would shut up, my chest is beating fast, I've made those mistakes he made, so....Just shut up! Does he think everybody wants the same salvation he's got? Ok, so I am lost, but if he'd just shut up I could go home! Doe he know I don't want to go to Hell? Ok, if you'll shut up now I'll ignore this. He didn't shut until I walked down the aisle. When I knelt on the alter his testimony was shut up and his prayer and began.

When God gives us something it will not be appreciated by all, and sometimes seems nobody appreciated it. We must do it anyway. We owe it to God. Not all appreciate Jesus' death on the cross, and he still loved us enough to do it. The son of God died for our sins and many don't appreciate it! We would be fools to think our meager efforts are going to be widely accepted or appreciated. We must do our little part. If in all years of our Christian live if we could be so lucky that 1 soul would walk down the aisle and meet Jesus because of our little seed. We have helped add to the number in Heaven, and that's worth it all.

What's Wrong With Us?
Sheppard, Teresa - TN

We Christians are not like those "sinners"! We are different. We have been saved by God's Grace. The Bible talks about us being a separated people. I agree that once we have been saved by God's Grace that it is eternal. I agree that we are different from other "sinners", but only because we know we are going to Heaven.

We should indeed be a separated people, but it makes me sad to realize just how much of the world we take part in. I say we because I've found I am no exception. Are you saying "well, not me!?" Thinking to yourself about how you don't drink, curse, go to bars, and how FAITHful you are to your spouse. Yeah, those are all good things, but there's more to being a Christian than the church covenant. It's with much discomfort I have to write these things. Most of you will still disregard these words, but as for me – God will not allow it.

What am I talking about? I am talking about the things that are wrong with us. Yeah, us the born again body of believers. God's church. "The Church". Let's look at some issues together.

1.) St. Patrick's Day. We dress up in Green, pinch others who don't participate, and have a few laughs. What's wrong with that? Do you know what you are celebrating?

2.) Witchcraft. This is familiar scripture: Galatians 5:19-21 *"Now the works of the flesh are manifest, which are these; Adultery, fornication, uncleanness, lasciviousness, Idolatry, witchcraft, hatred, variance, emulations, wrath, strife, seditions, heresies, Envyings, murders, drunkenness, reviling and such like: of the which tell you before, as I have also told you in time past, that they which do such things shall not inherit the kingdom of God."* Witchcraft? That's not an issue now days, right? It is an issue. What do you think our children are learning to believe in when they watch movies portraying sorcery, witches, Gods, and wizards? These movies entice our children and pollute their minds.

3.) Halloween. Oh, my goodness! Halloween is harmless. Why shouldn't we celebrate that? Do you know much about Halloween? I thought it was harmless too, in fact until recently I always participated in it. I was led by the spirit to stop observing Halloween. Halloween began with a people called Celtics. Celtics were ruled by Druids. The Druids were priest. (Popular belief is that these people believed much like Pagans) They lived 2,000 years ago in the area that is now Ireland, the United Kingdom, and Northern France. The Celts believed that the night before New Year, the boundary between the worlds of the living and the dead became blurred. On October 31st they believed the ghosts of the dead returned to earth. Celts taught that the presence of other worldly spirits made it easier for the Druids to predict the future. On this day people made sacrifices unto the Druids. How then did Halloween become so commercial?

136

How did it become so popular? There are religious groups that have adopted the holiday. Because of their acceptance and MONEY this holiday is huge! Research shows that the spending on Halloween is only second to Christmas. Mega Bucks! Don't worry though. We "saved, converted, born again people" we can keep on celebrating. There is some groups protesting the holiday. Guess Who? The Wican and Pagan Subcultures, because they view it as a religious holiday! What is wrong with us?

4.) Christmas. Of course we must celebrate Christmas! Christmas is the celebration of the birth of our Lord and Saviour Jesus Christ. I agree with that completely. Why then do we teach our kids to believe in Santa Clause? It's easy to get caught up in this. My 4 year old son knows Santa is pretend, but he's seen all the movies. I even paid for a picture with him and Santa. What is wrong with us? Look at Santa a little closer. Do a little research into what you celebrate when you celebrate Santa. I think you will be astonished at your findings.

5.) Marriage. Oh I know we Christians are opposed to same sex marriage. We have stood firm on this issue, but is that the only issue we are firm on? I read a shocking statistic it said this "24 % (percent) of all those currently in a relationship say honesty about finances is more important than honesty about fidelity," Wow! Two things are disturbing about that. 1) It says people in a relationship. It no longer matters if people actually bother to get married or not, and 2.) The obvious one, that they would rather their spouse (or whatever) to be honest about money than be FAITHful. I wonder how many Christian's have thought "I'd rather him/her cheat on me than take the money."

What is wrong with us? Why aren't our loved ones being saved? They aren't being saved because of what's wrong with us. What's wrong with us? We do not have enough separation from the world. We are the temple of the Holy Ghost of Jesus Christ. We are his church. We should not pollute his church. What's wrong with us? St. Patrick's Day, Evil movies, Halloween, Santa Clause. These things are just the beginning of what's wrong with us. We use our churches for un-holy events, we use them as a place for merchandise, we use them as a networking group, we use them as a social club, and gossip outlet. What's wrong with us? You decide. Pray, ask God for dance. I myself am no exception to such sins. I sin daily just as the rest of you. You would think that since God gave me such strong convictions about these things I would be knowledgeable on staying "separated from the world". Wrong. I've been participating in Yoga for about 2 years. Big deal? It is a big deal. It's a form of worship. Yoga originated in India. Yoga means Yoking union. The ultimate purpose of Yoga is to make our flesh and spirit become one with the inner "divine" being. There are many different denominations as with all beliefs. The common belief is that we each possess a divine being. We are all Deity. (This is at least my meager understanding of the practice.) What is wrong with us? How could I do that? Why all of a sudden did I decide to research Yoga? God convicted my heart. My Bible says: 1. Corinthians 15:50 *"Now this I say, brethren, that flesh and blood cannot inherit the kingdom of God; neither doth corruption inherit incorruption."* What's wrong with us?

Oh Lord, In thee I Understand
Teresa Sheppard – TN

My Pockets are empty, Oh Lord in thee I understand.
My home is divided many ways, Oh Lord in thee I understand.
{*"These things I have spoken unto you, that in me you might have peace. In the world ye shall have tribulation, but be of good cheer, I have overcome the world" John 16:33*} Oh Lord in thee I understand.
{*"Not because I desire a gift: but I desire fruit that may abound to your account" Phil 4:17*} Oh Lord, in thee I understand.
{*"Seek ye first the kingdom of God and his righteousness, and all these things shall be added unto you. Take therefore no thought for the morrow: for the morrow shall take thought for the things of itself. Sufficient unto the day is the evil thereof"* Matt 33-34} Oh Lord, in thee I understand.
My heart is full of joy, Oh Lord, in thee I understand.

A Conversation
Sheppard, Teresa – TN

Two friends were sitting together talking. We will call them 1 and 2. 1.) I try my best but I am not appreciated. 2.) What makes you think that? 1) Nobody listens to me they just make fun of me. 2.) Do you really believe that? 1.) Yes! It's true just the other day I invited my waitress to church and she laughed at me. 2.) Are you sure she was laughing at you? 1.) She smiled and said I seen her chuckling with her co-workers. Everyone make fun of me like that. 2.) My friend sometimes they do make fun of you, but not this time. In your anger you quickly placed your credit card in the money holder and didn't' read the note on the back of your receipt. Don't worry I read it. 1.) What note, what did it say? 2.) It said "Thank You! I really means a lot when God sends his people to me. I needed it. Thank You and may God bless you all." 1.) I've been such a fool. 2.) I always listen to you. Keep the FAITH. There are lots of times the world will reject you but remember why your are doing it. John 3:13-14 *"Marvel not, my brethren, if the world hate you. We know that we have passed from death unto life, because we love the brethren. He that loveth not his brother abideth in death."* Who were these people? 1.) A Christian 2.) Jesus

The Superbowl of Life
Sheppard, Teresa – TN

For a minute pretend your life is the last quarter and the last play of the Super bowl. The game is tied. This time there is a lot more than a ring to gain or lose. It's all up to you. Each team only has 4 players not including you. You are the ball. Yes, you are the ball. Doesn't it always seem that the ball, the referees, the announcers, and everything else are stacked in favor of one team versus the other? I think so. Therefore, you the ball are playing for the offensive tea. You will decide the fate of the game. The offensive players are: Preacher (Playing Quarterback), Jesus (Playing Running back), Angel (kicker) and Christian-1 (Playing the rest of the team). The defensive players have no set positions and all just run for the ball. The defensive players are: Satan, Demon (Satan's angel), Money (the most beloved player), and finally Christian-2 (aka out of God's will or stumbling block. The quarterback has called the winning play and it is all up to you. The quarterback passes the ball to the running back. The pass is ......Good! The running back has the ball. Christian-2 falls down on the field he's in the running back's way.

Wow look at that….Christian-1 is lifting Christian-2 up out of the way. Super bowl history has been made here today. The offensive team is picking up the defensive team! The running back is a the 20, the 10, the 5 and now bal it's all up to you. What can the ball do? Be still, hold tight, and let God move! Don't wiggle around just stick close to Jesus and let him run with you. No defense in the world can stop you from Heaven when Jesus is carrying you across the field. Just be still! You decide to win – Great! The ball and the running back are as one. The ball is not moving the pass the 5 and it's a TOUCHDOWN! You have won the Super bowl of life. Heaven will be your home. You get to live in a mansion, walk on streets of gold, and be in the presence of all the host of Heaven for all eternity. Don't be sad because the game is over. Rejoice for the celebration has just started! Good thing you chose to win. The loosing team is going to live eternity in the blazing hot fire of Hell! Just so you know, not making a choice is choosing to loose. The choice is yours. St. John 10:28-30 *"And I give unto them eternal life; and they shall never perish, neither shall any man pluck them out of my hand. My Father, which gave them me, is greater than all; and no man is able to pluck them out of my Father's hand. I and my father are one."*

Stuffed Shirts
Sheppard, Teresa – TN

Why don't you go to church? *I don't like those stuffed shirts.* Why? *You know those preachers with their stuffed shirts. Them fellars don't care 'bout nuthin' but filling the pews so they can fill their pockets.* Do you suppose all preachers is that way? *They surely are. You ever seen one of "em out to visit folks or trying to help anyone besides themselves? I'll answer for you, NO you ain't!* Well Now….. *Don't well me. We both know them so called "preachers" wouldn't care a bit if all us "lower income" folks just didn't exist at all. Did you know my wife's real sickly. Think God sent somebody to see about her? Because I'll tell you what I…..*Before you go any further, let me introduce myself. I'm the preacher from the little church down the road. I heard your wife was sick. God sent me to see about her and you. *You! You are a preacher! You don't look like* one of them *stuffed shirt fellars. God really sent you to us?* I am a servant to God. Not all preachers are stuffed shirts, and not all stuffed shirts want to fill their pockets. The good Lord knows what each of us needs. He puts his servants where we fit and where we can do the most for him. *I'm a good laborer on this farm you think your Lord would have a place for me.* Well the Lord Jesus said (Matt 9:37-38) **"Then saith he unto his disciples, *"The harvest truly is plenteous, but the labourers are few. Pray ye therefore the Lord of the harvest, that he will send forth labourers into his harvest."***

All Alone
Sheppard, Teresa – TN

I've felt so all alone. In a large room full of people I've felt so I'll alone. In my home with my family I've felt so all alone. In my workplace busy with phones and noisy co-workers I've felt so all alone. In the middle of the night the minutes seem like hours, I've felt so all alone. Sitting here on this pew with these people I've never felt so all alone. Jesus is knocking on the door of my heart. He offers to be my friend. If I let him in never again will I feel so all alone. {Mark1:5 *"The time is fulfilled, and the kingdom of God is at hand: repent ye, and believe the gospel"*}

FAITH
Sheppard, Teresa – TN

We seem to put all of our FAITH in this world and the people in it. How long is it going to take us to realize that the more trust we have in this world the more we will be let down. The world will come to an end. The people in this world are human they will fail you. You could spend your entire life depending on one person, what happens when you realize they are not perfect, or when they die. What do you do when the person you love more than God fails you? Where do you turn to? When you need money for food, when tragedy strikes, when your loved ones are sick? Who do you call upon? What do you do when the person who taught you about FAITH seems to have lost theirs? For each and every struggle every day of your life where do you turn? Most importantly where is your FAITH going to be when judgment day comes?

FAITH in God is the key to everything in life. Every moment every second, every day all the time. Beginning to the end the key to life is FAITH in God. We should rely on God for everything every day of our lives. God loves us! God will provide our every need. We shouldn't let this world get us down. We should put God first and remember why we are here. This world is not our home and this world is not the end of us. Let us not forget we are the children of God almighty! The Alpha and Omega! Do you think that the children of God should have need of anything? If we will only believe God will provide for us. We must believe and ask! God wants to help us. God is our heavenly father. None of us are worthy, but he loves us anyway. The Bible says if we have the FAITH of a mustard seed we could move mountains. We can't pick up and choose the parts of the Bible we believe. We must read it spiritually and believe it wholly. Every word we must hide in our hearts as the truth, because it is the truth. The way the truth and the life. It is our instruction manual to live by. We need to bring back our FAITH in our God.

Before you call a doctor, before you worry about a bill being paid, before you call upon your government assistance, before you worry if your soul might go to Hell, call upon God. God is the answer! We must have FAITH. FAITH is all that is real. It is the only thing we really own. FAITH is the key to peace. FAITH is the only way to survive. Our days in this walk of life are full of tribulation. We must keep our FAITH in God. Follow the ways of Jesus. Look to Job (A book in the Bible). Job's a great example of a man who kept his FAITH. Before all else fails and once all else fails God is there. FAITH. Above all I am thankful for FAITH. We receive our FAITH when we become a child of God. We become a child of God by accepting Jesus Christ as our personal Saviour. We do this when the spirit draws us and we believe that Jesus will save us from Hell. If you want FAITH and you have not been saved you can get it! Pray to God, get yourself a King James Version Bible, find a church that preaches from that Bible, and God will show you all you need to know about FAITH. FAITH only works if you believe. Most people believe(d) in Santa, the Easter Bunny, the Tooth Fairy, Superheroes, things that aren't real, why is it so hard to have FAITH in God that is real? Talk to God he will listen. You can have a personal relationship with God no matter who you are. Just pray. God is my father and he wants to be yours.

Do you believe?
Sheppard, Teresa – TN

Do you believe there is a God? Do you believe there is a Devil? Yes, of course you do. Knowing you believe there is a God and there is a Devil then surely you believe in Heaven and Hell. Yes, of course you do.

Knowing this you must believe God is love and all the that is truth and the Devil is Hate and the father of lies.

Do you believe I love you? Yes, you know I love you. Do you believe the church people love you? They really do! You do believe don't you? Yes, of course you can feel the church's love for you. We know that God is love and all love comes from God. So God gave me love for you, God gave the church love for you and God himself loves you! Do you believe God loves you? Surely you do.

Do you believe God sent his only son to die on the cross for your sins and mine? Yes, you do. I know it is hard to fathom, but you believe because you feel the power of the truth in God's Holy words. Do you believe in God's Grace. If you believe in God's grace and surely you do. You believe there's enough grace for every need. Precious saving grace. You believe, God's drawing your heart? What's stopping you from getting saved? {Romans 10:13 *"for whosoever shall call upon the name of the Lord shall be saved"*}

No One Will Know!
Sheppard, Teresa – TN

This is wrong, but no one will know! *A still small voice says "I am & I know"* Saturday night I will sing against nature, but Sunday I will be at church and no one will know.. *A still small voice says "I am & I know"* Saturday night I will party with the drunkards, but Sunday I will be at church and no one will know. *A still small voice says "I am & I know"* Saturday night I will commit adultery but Sunday I will be at church and no one will know. *A still small voice says "I am & I know"* Saturday night I will say hurtful and false things about my church family but Sunday I will be at church and no one will know. *A still small voice says "I am & I know"* Sunday I will go to church and pray with my brethren, and really be wondering what he did to be on the alter, but no one will know. *A still small voice says "I am & I know"* Sunday I will go to church pretend to hear the preached word, but thinking about how the preacher is wrong to say the words he's saying. No one knows the things I've done, he doesn't have the right to judge me. *A still small voice says "I am & I know"*

Someday soon I will go to judgment and meet Jesus, but I won't remember all that no one knew. *A still small voice says "I am & I know"* My reply is that's great! Then you know I always went to church, participated in all the church functions, and how I surely must have a grand mansion up here. The Jesus looks at me and says: Yes, you did attend church. You also committed sins against nature, partied with the drunkards, committed adultery, said hurtful and false things about my children, you judged my church and my preachers. Did you know not that works without FAITH is dead? Do you remember not when the pastor preached this sermon? In fact you did win souls, (My response, see I am good!) but, you won souls for Satan, go to continue to be one of his angels and with a final breath he said: "I never knew you; depart from me, ye that work iniquity." **Condemned to burn in hell for eternity, and no one will know!**

Going to Hell!
Sheppard, Teresa – TN

I thank God for the way he brings things to our attention. I've been praying that God would give me compassion for the lost. It's unfortunate, but us the "church" has favoritism. I greatly want to see all my family and friends saved. Yes I truly do, but what about the drug dealers, the gangs, and the prostitutes? Are we really concerned about them. Prior to the other day I would have said "I care about them". We should love and care as much about their salvation as we do any of our family. God showed me I didn't. I was visiting one of my little brothers. He said "I went to the funeral home last night." I said "Yes, I know the drug dealer that killed himself". I knew about it, but I hadn't cared about that man's soul. He said "Maybe, he didn't go to Hell. He lived 3 days after he stabbed himself." I said

" Well, only God knows." My brother who doesn't attend church anywhere and does not claim to be a Christian had a great concern and worry about this man going to Hell. Why didn't I care? That's something I have to pray to God about. Maybe God used this talk with my brother to open my eyes. I learned the next day that when this man stabbed himself while laying there in a pool of his own blood he wrote the words F- You in his own blood. I don't know where the scripture is, but the Bible says you can tell a tree by the fruit it bears. People really do go to Hell. Even the ones we love and maybe even you. It is my belief this man went to Hell. No one who had the love of God in their heart could have written that has they were dying. If you have not been saved you really are on your way to Hell. Hell is real and even if you're a good person you will go there if you haven't been saved.

Beans & Taters
Sheppard, Teresa – TN
Do you know what God did to me? It started at supper time. I had my food ready to eat. I was having beans, taters, macaroni, and dessert. I don't like for my food to touch. I put everything in separate little bowls. God dumped out my bows and stirred everything together!

Think of my meal as my life. My beans would be God as he should always be the main course (or most important) in our lives, the taters were my family and friends (always 2nd only to God.), macaroni was my career (important as to provide my needs, and finally my dessert is my church (A little treat that God gives us for strength and a way to see the lost saved.). As with my food I loved all the different parts of my life, but I've always kept them separate. All my life got stirred together when as ask God to put me in his will.

The Key
Smallwood, Gracie – VA
FAITH is the key that unlocks the gate in which your prayers go through.

Please Compare! (Written 06/23/1979 12:20 A.M.)
Smallwood, Gracie – VA

Many times you've heard it sang and countless times you've heard it told. The walls of jasper and the streets of pure gold. The rare beauty of that priceless city that shall unfold. It can not be completely told for eyes have not seen and ears have not heard what God as in store.

There is another place as well and many times you've heard of this place called "Hell". The one thing you know is its going to be awful hot there. But between Heaven and Hell, I'd like to mention of a few things to compare.

In Heaven there will be no need for the sun, moon, or stars for the Lord himself will light that city. In Hell light will never shine again for you'll be cast into outer darkness!

The children of God are looking forward to that meeting in the air for Jesus shall gird himself and serve his bride at the great marriage supper of the lamb. But in Hell you'll beg for just one drop of water, but there won't be any refreshments served! What about friends and loved ones? There won't be any friends or foe there everyone will be your enemy! There is weeping and wailing and gnashing of teeth! I am sure there won't be any socializing in that ferverant heat.

In Heaven there will be no pain, sorrow, sickness, or tears. Never a good bye spoken, no evil words, or hard feelings. For the heart there will never be broken. But in Hell there'll be tears of sorrow, regret and fear. There will be pain and utter despair, but did you know no one will care about your pain. I would like to tell you a few things you will never find and I mean never find. A Christian mother or saintly dad so dear, a darling little child will never be there. Never another smile upon anyone's face, not a sincere hand shake, no welcome mat, no kind neighbor to lend a helping hand, never a chance to make amends, no family gatherings for no doubt some of the family are home with God!

Never will you forget in former days the paths of sin you trod You trod. You had the opportunity but you turned your back on God!

The beautiful trees that grow on the hill as the wind softly blows springs flowers, the luscious grass where a child roams at will for all these things will be absent in Hell. In Heaven perfect peace and contentment! In Hell total confinement, pain, and darkness, but one thing there will surely be the greatest prayer meeting of all eternity. The saddest prayers that were ever prayed, but prayer time then will forever be too late! Oh, would you not rather kneel and pray today.

Just a Little Before You Do.
Smallwood, Gracie – VA

Each time there is a service in the church I attend, I love to get there early, just to welcome each one in. Just to know that you love Jesus and You've come to worship him. Oh how it thrills my soul to see the congregation gathering in. Ah! I want to get there early, just a little before you do. May he let me wait by the portals of glory as you pass through. Oh I want to see you smiling face as Heaven comes in view. Oh I want to get there early just a little before you do. Oh It's good to be in service in the house of the Lord. Just to praise his holy name and to feast upon his word. Oh to worship with God's children is the sweetest joy I know. I'm getting ready, ready to go.

Flowers Bloom (Written 09-13-1984 1:47 P.M.)
Smallwood, Gracie – VA

There are sweet flowers that bloom along life's way, but oh soon they are vanished away. It's like they have never been, but for in my heart, their beauty will never grow dim. Do you think when on the other shore they will shine forever more! Their beauty will shine forever more! Their beauty will never grow dim! Their fragrance and color will ever abide then. The leaves will soon turn now then fall to the ground. Time of summer flowers are almost past soon the snow will fall and cover the ground. Where are the flowers now you say? I think they are gone away for now they bloom still in my heart and mind, but in another land they are blooming in glory divine.

My Children (Written 04/17/1991 01:27 A.M.)
Smallwood, Gracie – VA

Children are a heritage of the Lord so the word of God does say. Bring them up in the way of the truth and right. Praying God will always keep them in his sight. My children have wondered so far, Lord, from you will they ever understand how much you love them the way you do? Lord help them to be able to see the way you made on Calvary! For it is the only way to make it to Heaven above. The price you paid in full by God's great love. You gave them to me dear Lord and now I give them back to you. Bring them by the way of the old rugged cross that their souls dear Lord won't be lost.

Time to Travel
Smallwood, Gracie – VA

You know the way is dreary, sometimes dark and cold. You know the burdens heavy that grips our very soul, but let me tell you brother, you don't walk alone. If you been saved and walking with Jesus, come on let's travel on. Come on weary pilgrim! Come on let's travel on! Come on weary pilgrim 'till we reach that land of song! Let he Saviour take your hand and live the best you can for our blessed Saviour let's keep on traveling on. When the Lord saved you dear sister he gave you job to do, don't sit there by the wayside feeling sad and blue. Put a smile upon your face put old Satan in his place, and come on dear sister, come on let's travel on!

Praying Through
Smallwood, Gracie – VA

We can come to the Lord in prayer, in sadness, and in joyful times. Learn to pray through. The strength, power, and encouragement received from the Lord while shut in with him must see you through the trials ahead. The victory you get in the secret closet has to give you victory oh the battlefield. Prayer is not finished until it sees you on the other side of your trials. The first way to learn to pray is by listening in prayer. Prayer is a 2 way road between you and God. The Lord will speak clear instructions to you. (Listen for him to speak.) Have total confidence in the word of God! Christ is the living word! The Holy Ghost will lead you to God's revealed word, while you are alone with God. So when you pray take paper, pen, and the word. Be ready to receive what the Lord is waiting to tell you. Put on the whole armour! Sword of the spirit act upon God's direction when he gives it to you! You want to talk to God? God wants to talk to you!

The Power
Smallwood, Gracie – VA

You can have power (electricity) in your home, but if you don't plug into it, or turn on the light you'll sit in darkness. Without the power we cannot work with our household tools. Are we not using the power in our lives that God has given us? Do we sit in darkness accomplishing nothing for God? When we can trust God completely we can thank him for the bad as well as the good. For he works it out for our good and his glory. He that is in you is greater than he that is in the world! The power of God in our lives is great than floods, hurricanes, tornados, and winds. God is all powerful and he lives in our body, spirit, and soul.

My Help
Smallwood, Gracie – VA

I will look to the hills, from whence cometh my help, My help cometh from the Lord!

Jesus Christ is Lord
Smallwood, Gracie – VA

He was born in a manger a long time ago. A new born baby you so often been told. He grew as a child, a boy and then a young man. They crucified him, buried him, but thank God he arose again! He lived, walked, talked, he had compassion on man! He ascended up to Heaven and sits at the right hand of God who sent him. I talk to him tell him of al the things that trouble and bother me. For he is my friend and he always stands for me! But it goes the other way as well you see, for Jesus talks to me! He tells me things to do to be a help to him, but do I listen to him as compassionately as he listens to me?

Expectancy
Smallwood, Gracie

The sun shines a new day begins with life all around, death is near but I won't fear for Jesus is just beyond. There before the thrown of God, we'll praise and honor him. I will sing so clear and ever praises ring! At the close of life's day and death draws near, I'll just close my eyes for Jesus is near. Hand in hand will cross the strand ever to be in glory land! Hand in hand we'll soar away to that land of eternal day! Peace, joy, and gladness of heart, my Lord and I never shall part!

Salvation For You
Smallwood, Gracie

If it were possible to take a look through the window of a sinner's soul what shocking sight to behold! For the camera of his mind places the ugly pictures on his heart of hate and greed, pride and deceit and misery and shame untold! A story true I tell, so listen as the scenes unfold. Comes a knock, knock upon the heart of that soul, as the door of his heart opens wide the pure love of God shines inside gone are the dark ugly scars of sin and now Jesus lives within! Now take a look and what do you see? A sinner saved by grace, so pure and clean. The scenery is changed he is not the same. He's all brand new! **What God did for him he can do for you!**

Gone Home! (Written 07/25/1991 01:40 A.M.)
Smallwood, Gracie – VA

When my family have done their best to properly lay my body to rest you will hear the announcement made of the day of my wake. No doubt you will want to come to say your good-byes and comfort my family and tell them of our times together rejoicing in the Lord in days gone by. As you look upon me the last time you go by don't let a single tear drop fall just remember I am no longer in this shell of a body at all. This body that you see is no longer needed by me. I've taken my flight to another land and I am eternally by my master's right hand. The earthly body is one that brought me great pain. Bringing it under subjection to my heavenly father has brought me great gain! For FAITH in the precious blood that Jesus shed for me has brought me safely to the beginning of my eternity. My battles are over my earthly race is won! I this beautiful land, Oh I see the son! He's holding out his hands to welcome me n. No more battles with sin for through him I now win! The victory I have won for today the Lord called me home! Oh the glory I behold! Why I'm standing on that street of God! You know the one you have read and heard so much about. Oh halleluiah! I think I'll shout! Maybe I'll run a little too! I'll never get tired or old I got a brand new body for my soul. Tomorrow they will take my body and put it in the ground. I know it will hurt you for a while that I'm no longer around, but lift up your head and look to heaven above and remember my Saviour's great love. How he came and gave his life on that old rugged cross that through FAITH in him no one would have to be lost. I have found that FAITH in his sweet love and it has taken me to my home above. By the way your reservation can be made to come and see me here. For this is a land of no more tears there is a river that flows through this city so fair. Oh, the splendor there is over here. I'll be waiting to welcome you in. Jesus and me and so many friends. So you be good now and when your time comes that valley of death to walk through if everything is o.k. with you and Jesus there won't be anything to fear, cause he'll just take you from there to here.

Memories of Mama
Smallwood, Gracie – VA

Mama had a daily routine. She would arise early, roll up her sleeves and start a fire in the old cook stove. Then she washed her face, hands, and arms in cold water. Then down by her chair at the stove she'd bow and talk to God. About what I really don't know for I was too young to listen much then, but I'm sure she asked to keep us safe and free from sin.

Some of my first memories of Mama was how she loved to sing. She especially loved to sing when she swept the floor. Seemed to be her time to sing. I was the youngest of Mama's eight children. She worked very hard to care for her family. At age eight my dad went to be with Jesus my mom had to work even harder to keep us all together, but at the end of each day before going to bed we all knelt to pray.

Mama's gone to Heaven to be with Jesus. We were blessed to keep her for 103 years. The light of Jesus in her life helped me find and serve Jesus for myself and I'll soon go to be with her in rest. Thank God for all the wonderful mothers who are still here to love Jesus and help shine a light for all to see. So if your mom is gone or still here to help show you the way. Love her with al your heart for soon we are going that same way.

A Lonely Prayer
Smallwood, Gracie – VA

My heart was aching and lonely too. I feel defeated Lord in so many things I try to do. Sometimes I feel, Lord like you've went away and that you don't love me anymore. My God I'm crying out to you. Forgive dear Jesus and bring me joy a new. Sanctify me. Make me Holy and complete. Let me joyfully worship you again Lord and please make the devil retreat. For Satan is a liar and a deceiver he will always be. All the troubles, all the pains, all the lies he has been trying to get me to believe. He wants me to think I'll fail in everything I do. Praise God I know there is victory, sweet wonderful victory in you Lord.

At Calvary
Smallwood, Gracie – VA

It's not in the things you have. It's not in the things you do. It's not in the things you use. It's in the guilt you loose at Calvary. It's not how popular you may be. It's not in the beauty you may see. It's just simply surrender to the only one that can set you free at Calvary. What make a man is not all this mucho stuff. What makes a man is not acting like a tough man. A man rises tall when he is humbled at Calvary. It's not in the things he possess that makes him rich. The respect of all those who know him as such. In this pauper he'll always be, but when he yields his life and soul to Jesus he stands tall. Shaking off all guilt at Calvary. Rich not in worldly things, but rich forever in eternity for it is the precious blood of Jesus that will forever let the glad bells ring, because of Calvary.

What Will Your Answer Be? (Written 11-10-1980)
Smallwood, Gracie – VA

I would really like to know, just what that you would do if Jesus came to your house to spend some time with you. Would he be welcome your will you say "please go away, you know I love you, but come another day." You have a house within you, can you not see Jesus knocking at your door. Oh, so patiently "please let me in to live with you. I'll save your soul and give you peace. What will your answer be?

Ready for Jesus
Smallwood, Gracie – VA

The sun is slowly setting behind the mountain of time. Jesus will soon be appearing upon a cloud of white. Will we be ready to greet him? He could come night or day. He's coming. Yes, he's coming. He will call his bride away. Jesus I want to be ready to meet you. Ready to greet you. Jut lift up holy hands as you carry me away. Just want to tell you I love you. Praise the Lord I'm with your forever and ever starting today. Troubles and worries are behind me. Never an unkind word to hear. From now on and forever my precious Saviour is here. Glory to God in the highest praises to his dear name. Now and forever I'm home with Jesus. Praise you holy name.

When I reach Home (written 01-12-1980)
Smallwood, Gracie – VA

Just as soon as I reach home oh there I'll be! See that precious son of God that has done so much for me. That first tender touch, that first sweet time, will make my problems of this life worth while. For it won't be the surrounding that makes it Heaven to me. It's really not the sainted millions I'm longing to see. Not wading in the river or resting 'neath the tree, but it's on the face of my see Jesus that I'm longing to see. He is the one I want to meet. You may want to see that city or someone gone on before you. You may have many visions for when your reach that golden shore, walls of jasper the street of gold, the gates of pearls, all of these in all their splendor, but I want to see my Lord.

Who Am I?
Smallwood, Gracie – VA

Who am I, you might would say? You think you know me I would just say nay! The true me is living in this house of clay. You look upon the outside of the house I'm living in. You think I am fat, middle aged, and not very pleasant to behold. But you know me, for the Lord says so beautiful is my soul! You look on the outside God see within the thoughts that are right and love so bright. So clean is them sounds as gold so pure he knows I'm thin. You watch me struggle from day to day. A few pounds to loose when Jesus says look within and not without. It sure was good news so fat or thin with Jesus living in my house there is joy and peace and that is what Jesus is all about.

Out of the Valley
Smallwood, Henry - VA

God gave me two good arms and feet. Knowing this when I get in a valley I can lift my arms and feet for God and start climbing out of that valley. I tell the devil get behind me I ain't got time for you. {Author's Note: Henry really means this. He had throat cancer, but God gave him a full recovery and he never ceased his daily activity while being treated for cancer}

Ecclesiastes
Name Withheld – TN

Ecclesiastes is a book in the old testament. Ecclesiastes means preacher. I interpret this book as a sermon. The thought would be vanity. My meager understanding of the sermon is this "If it's not for God it's vanity". I agree with that. This flesh will perish. Therefore, anything of or relating to this fleshly life that does not involve God in the long run is useless. Yeah, I know we are all human and we will live as humans until we go home, but think about it. All the care we take of our flesh and the fun we pursue for our flesh – it's worthless. If we die unsaved we will still go to Hell. The pursuit of the Kingdom of Heaven and helping lead others there is all that really matters. Instead of quoting scripture I encourage you to read it. Read the book of Ecclesiastes in the Old Testament.

Do you Think About it?
Name Withheld – TN

It's the middle of the night and suddenly you find yourself awake. You jump from your cozy bed to check on your family. Oh, thanks be to God they are fine. Do you ever think about who it was that awoke you or why?

You are late for work and driving well above the speeding limit. All of a sudden something within tells you "slow down". You slow down just to find an accident or traffic delay right in front of you.

Glory be to God you slowed down. Do you ever think about who told you to slow down?

You are having financial troubles. You pray about. Before, you realize it your finances are fine again. Do you ever think about why it worked out?

You have so many blessing. You have so many gifts. Are you thinking I have nothing? I'm sure you are blessed. Do you have a place to sleep? Do you have a means of transportation? Do you have family? Are you healthy? Do you have electricity? Do you have heat? If you have any of these you are blessed. Most of you probably have them all. You have none of these? Have you been saved? Are you Lost? Whether you are lost or saved you are still blessed.

Yep, with none of the blessing listed and even without salvation you are blessed. Salvation is the greatest gift to us from God. If you are lost you are still blessed because God filled your body with breath another day so that you still have a chance to be saved. Will today be the day?

CHAPTER 5

SONGS & RESITATIONS

{Psalms 42:8 "Yet the Lord will command his loving-kindness in the day-time, and in the night his song shall be with me, and my prayer unto the God of my life."}

Our Churches
Pelfrey, Charlene - TN

A lot of churches today are run by man's way not God's way. They tell the singers what to sing and the sinners what to say. They try to light a fire without striking a match. They shut God out. Shut the door and left him outside. When he tries to get in they tune him out. It's time we open our eyes and let God have his way. Sinners are dying in this world every day. Back in better days two (2) preachers would preach at once while the singers were signing. There was shouting and praising his name. Time was something we never noticed a schedule was not kept. Sinner's we welcomed they were a special guest and their souls were getting saved.

Jesus Is Coming
Pelfrey, Charlene – TN

The sun will be darkened the moon won't give light. The stars will start falling and then what a wonderful sight. In his glory Jesus will appear on the same cloud he left on all those years ago. Jesus is coming, coming on a cloud. He done prepared mansion. He made his father proud. The way has been made for his children to come home. Oh, praise the Lord the time is almost here. The trumpet is now sounding. All the world can hear. Jesus has called us al who are saved. Come unto me. I've been waiting for this day for a long time.

Time to Change
Pelfrey, Charlene – TN

Have you ever watched a loved one die and heard them cry out in pain. Have you sat by your mom and dad and held their hand while they passed away. You knew deep inside their life wasn't over because the best was yet to come. For when the wake up what a glorious sight there is Jesus right by their side. That old shack where they lived in below is now a mansion and the streets are pure gold. There are angels all around them and there are sounds of lorry. All their pain is gone and now their finally home. Have you ever watched a sinner die in pain and sorrow with no hope in their eyes. Knowing they will never see their loved one's again. They think this is just the end. For when they wake up in pain and torment and the flames are all around them and they are burning from within. Have you ever wondered how many father's and mother's have woke up in Hell screaming just to see that there children had followed them in. Not only will they burn but they have to watch their children burn. Please don't let this happen to you. There's time right know to change. Ask the Lord to save you and bring your family in. Then we will be in Heaven together and walk with Jesus hand in hand and live there forever in God's Glory.

Dad
Pelfrey, Darrell - TN

He was only here for a little while but now he's gone. He was my dad and I remember the hard times he had. I know he's alright no more suffering or pain because he walking with Jesus side by side. I believe he's looking forward to what day when we all come that way. I still think about him every day and the pain he went through. One day when it comes my time I will be ok to. Because we will be walking with Jesus Dad and me. He was only here for a little while but now he's gone. We will be walking with Jesus for eternity. Lovingly dedicated to Herbert Eugene Pelfrey. Author's Note: Darrell Pelfrey the author of this song is my Dad. Growing up I never would have thought he'd be writing gospel music. I am however, thankful that he is.

The Only Way
Pelfrey, Darrell – TN

With his eye's toward heaven and a tear on his face forgive them father was the words he prayed. Nailed to a cross with three old rusted nails, made by man and drove with his hands. His blood dripping down from the spear in his side but still he prayed with tears in his eyes. You see this man was Jesus he died for our sin's he gave all he had for you and me. So don't waste no more time with what this world has to give our time here is short in heaven you can live. So remember what he's done for you, he died on that cross he love you enough to shed his blood for you. You see this man is Jesus he's here with us today believing in him is the only way. With his eyes toward heaven and a tear on his face forgive them father was the words he prayed. You see I have not always been a good man I had trouble in my life but I always knew he was there. I was never along. You see this man was Jesus he's here with us today believing in him is the only way. The only way, the only way, the only way, the only way. With his eyes toward heaven and a tear on his face forgive them father was the words he prayed.

Run to the Rock (Written in 1993)
Smallwood, Gracie -VA

{Verse 1}The storm clouds are gathering. The mighty billows going to roll and you are in danger of loosing your soul: There is only one way to make it thru: Run oh Run to Jesus so True.

{Chorus} Run oh run to the rock of ages: He is the shelter from the storm: Run oh run to the rock of ages: By the blood, hide in Jesus' arms.

{Verse 2} When life is over, darkness appears and the moon dripping blood, Oh what awful fear, too late you'll hear. You've already lost your soul.

{Verse 3} There's no coming back for another chance, your soul from Hell to save, you'll forever be lost, but Christ paid the cost, to spare you this fate.

{Verse 4} The billows are rolling, the dark clouds are gathering: Your soul is in danger today: Please heed the warning before the Saviour is coming to take his bride away.

{Verse 5} No way to get out of that awful place, while eternity rolls, year after year, day after day, Such pain and sadness. Oh such darkness and fear!

Praise the Lord (Written in 1985)
Smallwood, Gracie –VA

{Verse 1} I just want to lift up holy ands and praise the Lord; Lift up holy hands and praise the Lord! Won't you stand to your feet, lift up holy hands and praise the Lord, Praise the Lord, Praise the Lord.

{Verse 2} Thank you for your blessings, your kindness and your love! We feel your presence coming from above, flowing through our midst and it makes me want to say; Praise the Lord! Praise the Lord!

{Verse 3} We've gathered here to honor and adore you; to praise and worship before you. For you are Lord of Glory, King of Kings and we adore you! Praise you forever and ever, Praise the Lord.

When FAITH Becomes Reality
Smallwood, Gracie – VA

Heaven is so real to me…for I grasp my dreams by FAITH you see. FAITH in Christ who saved my soul from sin. For when my eyes shall look upon all he has built for me… my FAITH has then become. reality. God's love is so real so sweet and true was sent to us through Christ. God's perfect gift to you. By FAITH I received this gift and the benefits of his love. When FAITH becomes reality I'll be enjoying my home above. When I look upon his precious face When I have finally run this race, when I can hear my blessed Saviour say to me " My child you may enter in! For the crown of life you now win! You rant he patience will for me." It's then my FAITH will become reality. Reality. Reality. When my FAITH has become reality. I'll be singing in Heaven's choir looking upon the one that I admire. Forever to worship and adore my king of kings. Reality. Reality. Then my FAITH has become reality.

Cast Your Bread Upon the Waters.
Smallwood, Gracie – VA

Cast your bread upon the waters, Jesus seems to say. Have FAITH and trust me for there is no other way. My word will do what it was sent to do, and if you'll trust me I will see you safely through.

Look all around my child at the world you're living in. It has grown so wicked and so full of sin. Darkness is all around you, but help is from above, and I'll take you away of the wings of love!

(Chorus) Cast your bread upon the waters, Jesus seems to say. Have FAITH and trust in me for there is no other way. My word will do what it was sent to do and if you'll trust me I will see you safely through! Cast your bread upon the waters and worry not I say. Do all you have to do and say all you have to say. Do it all in a hurry for I'm surely coming soon. Cast your bread upon the waters and it shall return to you!

My Eternal Trip
Smallwood, Gracie – VA

The moon will be no stopping place when I leave this world. I'm going far beyond the stars for this I surely know. I've a home prepared for me away up in the sky. I'm just waiting now you see to be transported there on high. When the prince of peace shall step out from his home above. Then I know I'll understand the meaning of his love. His marvelous face I shall behold and forever be in the likeness of my Lord throughout eternity. When the Eastern sky shall open wide and the son of man appears. He'll step out on a great white cloud and all the saints shall hear. The most beautiful words we have ever heard and long we've waited for. To hear our blessed Saviour say my chi dome on up here.

My Friend Jesus (Written 11-04-1972)
Smallwood, Gracie - VA

When I go through the valley low, as I climb the mountain steep. Bearing the burdens of this life bitter tears I weep, but whether I go through the valley low or climb the mountain high, I've got a friend yes a friend who is always by my die. Who's that friend, Praise God it's Jesus! Did you say it was Jesus? Oh yes It's Jesus! Do you mean King Jesus? Glory Glory it's Jesus. Hallelujah it's Jesus and he will stand by me. There's a man yes a man who calmed the raging sea, fed the hungry and healed the sick, he made the blind to see, and the things he did then he can do now. When I'm nearing the end of my journey here below and I come to the river of Jorden He'll be there to show the way across the valley of death an onto Heaven's shore there. Praise God I'll be with him, there forever more.

Be Happy In Jesus
Smallwood, Gracie – VA

Be happy in Jesus this very day. Rejoice in him in every way. He is the one who saved us from sin and he is the one who dwells within. Be happy in Jesus in all that you do. Be happy in Jesus let his love shine through. In your work in our play praise our Lord in every way. No matter what trials comes our way. Be happy in Jesus for he is our stay. Our way. Be happy in Jesus in all that you do. He is the one that will take you through this troubled world. Day by day he'll take your hand and he'll lead the way. Be happy in Jesus let it show through in all that you say and all that you do. Don't murmur, don't worry, or complain for Jesus will take care of everything. Al of our problems are for a short while remembering this should bring a great smile. Let the glory that comes from within shine on your face. It's ;the love beams of Jesus shinning through. Every promise he made he will do.

We Won
Smallwood, Gracie – VA

We're on the winning side. We're on the winning side. Just like Elijah we're on the winning side. I will not loose. I'm on the winning side. I can not loose got Jesus by my side. In the caves of doubt or the valley of despair I'm on the winning side. God is always there. I'm on the winning side. You're on the winning side. We won. WE won. We won. Praise God we won!

By the Blood of the Son (Written in 1996)
Smallwood, Gracie - VA

1) There's a wonderful and beautiful city to enter when life's work is done. Our hope is to live in that city. No one enters, but by the blood of the son. Chorus) By the blood of the son, at Calvary by the blood of the son. There's an entrance for me. Oh what cleansing and power to set free, oh praise is name, the way was made at Calvary!

2.) By the blood of the lamb, by Jesus who died! By love my Saviour was crucified by his loving power God raised him again, Oh Praise the Lord, I can live with him.

Omega (Written in 1991)
Smallwood, Gracie – VA

Time to fly away on the wings of love. Fly high to that heavenly Dove! He is calling from far away. He's calling me to that land of eternal day.

My love, my dove, my precious friend, I reach out to you to take my hand; to console me & enfold me in your mighty arms. Eternally safe from every harm. My eternity begins, where voices blend in perfect harmony. Praising my King as the angels sing. Perfection like I've never known. I sail through the blue, as I bid you adze, I'm going home where I never roam. As the sweet angels sing, the heaven will ring with praises to the lamb. Glory to God, I now can trod on the golden sands of heavens shores. My love will hold me forever more.

Flowers Bloom (Written in 1984)
Smallwood, Gracie – VA
There are sweet flowers that bloom along life's way, but oh so soon they are vanished away. It's not like they have ever been, for in my heart; there beauty will never grow dim. Do you think when on the other shore they will shine forever more? Their beauty will shine forever their beauty will never grow dim. Their fragrance and color will ever abide. The leaves will soon turn and fall to the ground. The time of summer flowers are almost past. Where are the flowers now you say? You think they're gone away. In my heart and mind in another land they are blooming in Glory divine.

Let Me Lean On You Lord (Written in 1997)
Smallwood, Gracie – VA
Let me lean on you Lord, let me lean on you, when I'm feeling low and weary and I don't know what to do, Let me lean on you Lord, just to let me lean on you. Let me feel your precious presence flowing through me. Guide me by you high Lord then I can surely see. Let me lean on you Lord, let me lean on you. When I feel I'm about to stumble Lord I would surely fall, without your arms around me I couldn't stand at all. I feel your precious presence, just hovering over me and your blessed face I soon shall see. Let me lean on you Lord, let me lean on you!

Every-body Ought To Know
Smallwood, Gracie – VA
Everybody ought to know who Jesus is. Everybody ought to know what the Bible says. He is Alpha and Omega the beginning and the end. Everybody ought to know who Jesus is. Everybody ought to know who Jesus is. Everybody ought to know what the Bible says. He's the beautiful rose of Sharon, the bright and morning star. Everybody ought to know who Jesus is. Everybody ought to know who Jesus is. Everybody ought to know what the Bible says.

I am the I am the God of Abraham. Everybody ought to know The Great I am! Everybody ought to know who Jesus is. Everybody out to know what the Bible says. He is the lily of the valley. The lamb forever more. He is the king of kings and Lord of Lords. The great I am – God of Abraham, the one that I adore.

CHAPTER 6

ALL ABOUT THIS BOOK

Faith is our key to surviving this life. In St. John 16:33 Jesus said *"__These things I have spoken unto you, that in me ye might have peace. In the world ye shall have tribulation, but be of good cheer: I have overcome the world.__"*

The Creation of This Book

FAITH wrote this book. I rededicated my life to Jesus and I ask him to give me a job to do. Yes, I wanted to work for my Lord. The first thing the Lord ever laid upon my heart to write was "Dear Jesus". I wrote a few others after that.

I was having trouble at work. It seemed I worked so much I had no time to work for God. I felt like I was in bondage. I just couldn't understand why God would give me so much zeal and no time to use it. I tried to make an agreement with my boss to work part-time. That didn't work out. During that time my husband was very sick. He was in the emergency room several times before the problem was solved. I came into work late one morning (after having spent the previous night in the emergency room with my husband) my boss was angry. He made it clear that if I was going to work for him he had to be my first priority. He also reinforced my need for the job as I was making a very good living. (I had the greatest feeling of peace that come over me.) I knew God would help me. My priorities are God, family, and then my career. My boss even went as far as to offer me counseling. I lost my job. I am not angry with that employer. I even understand the way he felt. I just wish he could understand my FAITH. I know that job is not where God wanted me. While I was sitting in his office listening to him tell me how I needed that job I remembered a sermon from the preacher. It was how God is our provider. I walked out the door of that office with a smile on my face and peace in my heart. Which seems crazy to some because I have a mortgage, a child, and spouse that depend on my income. I had no clue what was going to happen next.

The day after being fired I went to copy shop to fax off a resume. In the parking lot my son called my grand-mother from my cell phone. We began to talk. I told her of the things that were going on. She had some very encouraging words. She even told me that she writes things for God. I knew I had to go see her. I never went into the shop to fax that resume. At that time I was thinking maybe we'd just make copies of the things we'd written and pass them out. She lives in Virginia and I in Tennessee. I got up early the next morning and headed off to visit her. It was one of the best spirit filled days I've ever had. She said God would provide for me. When I came back from her house I found a letter in my mailbox. It was a job offer from Sentry Insurance! Praise God! It was and is an even better job than the one I had before. Sentry is an amazing company and they by the grace of God have given me an excellent opportunity. I am free to make my own schedule! I don't want to sound like a commercial, but Sentry insurance is the greatest insurance company in the world! I am thankful for the way God put Sentry in my life.

Things were getting back on track. Then it happened.... The Lord he laid it upon my heart to write a book. My reaction "What, how?" That same day I picked up my copy of "Singing News" a gospel singing magazine and there it was! It was an advertisement for Xulon Press a Christian publishing company. I said ok, Lord I'll call them. They sent me a brochure. I prayed again "Lord, I don't know even know how to type a manuscript" Again, I was doubting what God was leading me to do. I looked down and there was directions to a link on Xulon's website. This link contained detailed instructions on how to type a manuscript! Thus the book began. A few months went by and I had done very little work on the book. I began to feel an urgency to complete the book. I didn't have nearly enough testimonies and I didn't have the money to publish the book. I being doubtful again, prayed "Lord, you know my needs I don't know how I'm going to pay for this.....please help me. It's amazing I didn't tell one soul that I needed the money to pay for the book. All I did was pray that prayer. The very next day the good Lord provided a way for me to pay for the publishing of the book!

This is the Lord's project so I know in my heart that any money earned from this project belongs to him. I found that I needed to establish a non-profit organization in order to properly care for the Lord's money. I didn't know how to do that either. God made it work out simply and easily. I didn't even have to hire a lawyer. God taught me everything I needed to know as I needed to know it. I didn't do this alone. God was with me every step of the way, and he sent me Christian helpers! I appreciate all the efforts, donations, prayers, and people willing to follow the spirit of God.

I had to have trustees for the non-profit group and God laid some people on my heart. They were very kind in agreeing to help. What's more than that is they have been a tremendous help to me with this project. I praise God for the help he sent! I would have been to independent to ask for help, but the trust required it. Thank God! I started working on the book in September of 2005. March 15, 2006 it was submitted to the publisher. That's only six (6) months! I think somewhere the Bible says little is much when God is in it.

FAITH CHARITIES

FAITH Charities is the name of the non-profit trust created because of this book. This is God's project and the money will be used to further God's work. Here is a brief biography on each of the trustees for FAITH Charities.

Corum, Miranda

My name is Miranda Corum. I was born February 19, 1980. I was raised in Luttrell, Tennessee. I was saved a few years ago. I've got a husband and two (2) children. I am a nurse at a local nursing home. My home church is Mountain View Church of God of the Union Assembly. That is where I teach Sunday School to three (3) – six (6) year olds. I would like to thank God for the many blessings he has sent my way. I am thankful for this book that he has placed on Teresa's heart and each and every testimony that was given. May God bless you all. {Author's Note: Miranda is a dear friend and blessing from God. The first time I heard her testimony I knew God had a special purpose for our friendship. Miranda is kind, patient, and caring. The greatest thing I've noticed about Miranda is she knows how to stand still and let God move. I know God chose her to be a trustee. I believe she will always wait upon the Lord before making any decision about this charity.}

Dyer, R. Jason Rev.

I was born on August 9th, 1976 in East Tennessee. I have always lived in the same rural community in Union county all of my life. I got saved and became a born again child of God in 1988. I graduated high school. I have worked at the same place for ten (10) years. I was married in 1998 to my wife (Amy). Our only son (Jaimen) was born in 2002. I accepted the call from God in 1996 to preach his word. I was ordained in 1997 and pastored for the first time that year. I currently pastor a church where I have pastored since 1998. I was raised in a loving, strict, & Godly home. I am thankful for my Christian raising. I love the Lord because he first loved me. I love serving the community and the church I attend. I am forever grateful to God for his Mercy and blessings to me and my family. I hope that this book will bless you and help you along life's way. God Bless you! {Author's Note: Jason is one of the most unique people I've ever met. Though he is human, his love and commitment to God are the greatest I've ever seen. He's been my pastor for about two (2) years. The Bible talks about a pastor watching over the flock, and he really takes that to heart. Jason and Amy made a special effort to welcome us (as with everyone) into the church. They consider the church members not only friends, but family. Jason's love for people doesn't stop in the church. He is active in the community and well loved. His spirit is impossible to describe. Jason is one of those people you just can't keep from loving. Jason & Amy are both a blessing to the community and our little church. I am thankful God chose him as one of the trustees. His Godly leadership will be important to this project. }

Sheppard, Teresa

I was born December 28, 1976. I live in Knoxville, Tennessee. I was raised in a poor, but Godly home. I was saved when I was young. I graduated from high school and attended a community college. I want to be a full-time solider for God, but my career is in the insurance industry. My husband (Vance) and I have one (1) son (Alex.). I am thankful that God saves us into a good work. God blessed me with the work of this book and charity. I am currently a member of Blaine's Chapel Missionary Baptist Church. The church is a blessing to me and I am thankful to be part of a growing church that allows the spirit to flow freely.

Smallwood, Gracie

My name is Gracie Taylor Smallwood. I was born in a coal mining town in South West Virginia. I married at fifteen (15) years old. I had my first child at age seventeen (17). By the time I was twenty-nine (29) I had seven (7) children. I was saved at age eight (8). You will find several things I've written and I feel so blessed to be able to share what God has given me. I wrote my first song in 1970. I written many things since then. I wondered why God kept giving me things to write down that weren't being used. I kept them in a file cabinet all through the years. God had a plan. My grand-daughter is such a blessing to me and I thank God for this opportunity. {Author's Note: Gracie is mamaw to me (my grand-mother). She wasn't part of my life until I entered my early twenties. I am so thankful I've had the blessing of getting to know her. She is truly a prayer warrior. She is strong in the FAITH. Though she had little formal education she is amazingly smart and resourceful. I've never known a woman who knew so much about the Bible. I've never had a conversation with her that wasn't about the Lord. She like all of us has made mistakes in her life, but with God she has overcome the adversity. You would never dream a woman her age with that much spark and FAITH would have ever been through anything. She's had a treacherous life and perhaps that's why her FAITH is so strong. She didn't know it, but she started on this book six (6) years before I was born. This is her work from God as much as it is mine. I am so thankful for her.}

Special Recognition:
I believe in giving people flowers while they are living. God first and foremost deserves the honor and glory for all things. Thank you God for this book! A huge thank you and God bless you to all those who donated their stories. My little church Blaine Chapel Missionary Baptist has been a great help. I'm thankful to my parents (Darrell & Charlene Pelfrey) who raised me in a Christian home. I need to give a special thank you to a few of people.

Jack Hodge. God arranged my introduction to Mr. Hodge. He is a singer, songwriter, poet, artist, disc jockey, and host of a gospel television program. The greatest thing about Mr. Hodge is he is a soldier for God. He was very gracious in donating his written works. He went above and beyond by arranging book signings, providing additional places to sell books, and creating a web page for FAITH Charities. Mr. Hodge was a blessing from God and we are thankful for his obedience. Jack's effort for FAITH Charity has been free of charge. He knows the charity wishes to use any profit to glorify Jesus. Mr. Hodge currently has several works of his own in progress. For more information on Jack Hodge or his work:

Jack Hodge
P O Box 5623, Sevierville, TN 37864
E-Mail: glorylandhighway@msn.com
http://groups.msn.com/JackHodgeGospelSingingMinistries

Teresa Tate. Teresa is my aunt. My grandmother (her mother – Gracie Smallwood) told her all about the book and FAITH Charities. {For those of you that don't realize it FAITH Charities has to buy copies of this book to re-sale them on a local level. One-hundred percent (100%) of all funds raised through this book will be used to further God's work.} She was so proud of our effort she donated money so we would have books to re-sale! (This was a very big deal because FAITH Charities had very little money. We were waiting on God to provide us a way.) Her only request was that I would send her one (1) book and autograph it for her. Teresa is the kind of person you hope your kids will be. I am sure God knew she was a good example for kids and placed her in the school system as a teacher. She is one of those special teachers that goes above and beyond to make sure her students get a quality education in her classroom. She has a giving heart full of love and is always ready to help. Here are a few words to her "Aunt Teresa, I love you and thank you for your encouragement and donation. I know you weren't looking for public recognition, but I hope and pray you don't mind it. You are a blessing from God and I am very thankful to God for placing you in my life. With Love, Teresa Sheppard" In case you are wondering…. I was named after her.

Praise 96.3 & Jamie Lewis – Praise is a local radio station. They are the only radio source for Southern Gospel music in this area. Praise is my favorite station. I decided to go in there and see if there was anything they could do to help us get the word out about this book. As I was walking into the station I literally ran into Jamie Lewis. Jamie is the general sales manager for Praise. I didn't know who Jamie was at this point. Jamie stood there while I explained to the receptionist why I was there. The receptionist said "This is Jamie and she is whom you need to speak with however, she is on her way out." Jamie said "Wait, you can follow me out and tell me about what you are doing." I briefly told her about the book and Faith Charities. She said she would love to meet with me about it. We arranged an appointment. I met with Jamie and we talked for a couple of hours. She was full of ideas. She offered to give us (no cost!) an hour on 2 separate programs to promote the book. She said she was doing this 1.) Because we are local 2.) Because all of the proceeds are going to charity and 3.) Because she feels this book will be a blessing to people. She said she would love to enter her own testimony about coming to work for the station. Because of restraints on time she was not able to do this, but she did share the story with me. She worked for a large station in Knoxville, Tennessee. She was making a good income and happy with her career. As she became acquainted with Southern Gospel Music she loved it! She got to know all the folks at Praise. They offered her a job. She did not accept right away. This went on for three (3) years. She was driving one day and she said "The Lord audibly spoke to me and told me to go to work for Praise!" and that's how she came to work there. She took a big pay cut as Christian stations aren't as profitable as the others, but God has fully blessed and she has not suffered need. I am so thankful to the folks at Praise for their help. They are such a blessing to the community. They had no idea I was going to recognize them in the book in fact neither did I until the Spirit hit me as I was doing my final edit. To Jamie and all the folks at Praise "Thank You and God Bless You!" I hope we will be able to hear from Jamie in Volume 2.

God is FAITHful. He Keeps his Promises.
Smallwood, Grace – VA

My oldest daughter was diagnosed with stomach cancer in June of 1988. She took treatments at a hospital in Charlottesville, VA. I spent the whole day at the hospital and it was time for her husband and I to go back to the place we were staying. He ask if I would mind if he went to the recreation room. He needed to be with people. That was fine with me for I needed to pray. I needed to hear from the Lord.

I prayed (for how long I don't know.) Many prayers and tears later the Lord spoke to me through the Holy Spirit. This was the message "Look not to the left or the right, but keep you eyes on me and I will show you great and wonderful things that you have not yet seen." That was more than seventeen (17) years ago.

My thought form that prayer was maybe that my daughter would be healed of her cancer. She died about six (6) months after that prayer. I searched many times for the meaning of what the Lord had told me.

I believe the answer to God's promise is in this book. For what a great and wonderful thing it is to be able to tell what Jesus has done for me. This book will reach people around the world. I believe this is what his promise was about. I'm so happy to have a small part in this to the Glory of God my father and our Lord Jesus Christ. I praise God forever. My prayer in the writings in this book is that it will touch many hearts and lives. God only knows how far it will be. {Author's Note: Rev. Jason Dyer told me he had prayed to be a part of something great. Jack Hodge told me he had been praying for a way to publish more of his works. God answered our prayers and put us together.}

A NOTE TO THE READER.

As with most literary works this carries a language of it's own. I realize some of the wording may seem strange to those of you without the FAITH or a different religious background. The scriptures from the Bible are written in bold and italics. The scriptures spoken by Jesus are in bold, italics, and underlined. I have provided the definitions of a few things. I hope you will find these helpful and the book a blessing.

<u>Definitions</u>

Age of accountability – The time in ones life when God through the Holy Spirit show you that you are lost and are doomed for Hell if you are not saved.

Amen – 1.) To Agree (Example if you agree with a testimony or something the preacher is saying.) 2.) Let it be so. (When we pray we say "In Jesus Name, Amen" We pray in Jesus name because the Bible instructs us to ask in the name of the son, and then say amen, let it be so.)

Anoint – This is meant two (2) ways in the Bible. 1.) We anoint (put oil on) and pray as a sign of obedience for those whom are sick. 2.) It can be a spiritual (poured out on) anointing of the Holy Spirit. *I John 2:20 "But ye have an unction from the Holy one, and ye know all things."*

Denomination – The sign over the door of a place of worship that identifies the type of belief that is practiced there. There is one

God. "The Great I am". There is one word of God. St John 1:1-2 " *In the beginning was the word, and the word was with God, and the word was God. The same was in the beginning with God.*" How do we take from one word and direct it to so many meanings (denominations)? Regardless of denomination the Bible says that God's house of all nations shall be called the house of prayer. I look at denomination like a sign over a grocery store. I wouldn't know what the store was selling if they didn't have a sign. When picking a denomination look for the King James Version Bible.

Drawing Power – A feeling or urgency from God. Is almost indescribable. Your heart beats fast, you feel like a force (God) is telling you to go to the alter. (In the case of salvation) It's like you know God is showing you that if you don't go you will die and go to Hell.

FAITH – Hebrews 11:1 "*Now faith is the substance of things hoped for, the evidence of things not seen:*" To me FAITH is knowing without seeing and believing because of what you feel in your heart. FAITH is walking in the spirit and not the flesh. Hebrews 10:38 "*Now the just shall live by faith: but if any man draw back, my soul shall have no pleasure in him.*"

Grace – Grace is an unmerited favor. Unmerited means you can not earn God's favor. You don't have any way to do so. It is freely given by God. Grace is better felt than told.

Heaven – Heaven is a place of beauty. The eternal home of God's children. A place where there will be perfect peace. The Bible tells us that it is so beautiful that we can not comprehend it. On this side of life we will never fully understand what awaits us on the other side. To me the greater joy that will be is to be able to be with Jesus forever. How do you define Heaven?

Hell – Hell is a place of eternal punishment. There is no joy, no peace, and no relief in Hell. The Bible tells us a lot about Hell. There was a rich man who opened his eyes in Hell. He was in horrible head and darkness and not one drop of water. The most awful thing I think is that you will not have a chance to repent. God will forever turn his back on you. It will be forever too late to change things then. For eternity you'll still be burning in Hell. Hell is just as eternal as Heaven.

Hope – The feeling that what is desired is also possible or that the event may turn out for the best. A person n whom or thing in which expectations are centered. Romans 8:24 *"For we are saved by hope: But hope that is seen is not hope: for what a man seeth, why doth he yet hope for?"*

Mercy – Mercy means to exercise compassion. God's mercy stands in place of God's judgment. We deserve death but God gave Mercy through Jesus.

Mountain – Mountain appears many times in the Bible with different meanings. To most Christians a mountain represents a great battle we are facing. When we are rejoicing in the spirit of the Lord we feel as if we are on the top of the mountain. We feel we are on the mountain top when we through Jesus have conquered the valley.

Preacher –A person who preaches; especially a minister. A preacher, preaches the word of God explaining to others by the Spirit of God a message from God to us.

Redeem- To pay a ransom for/to purchase or to buy. To rescue.

Redeemer – The one that pays the ransom, the one that purchases or buys.

Revival – To be revived or renewed. A series of meetings for renewing interest in our religion. Sometimes we grow away from our Lord. We allow many things to come between us and our Lord. A revival can be a renewing of your relationship to God. A church revival where a group of people renew their relationship to God. It is also a great time to see souls saved.

Rock of Ages - Jesus is the rock in a weary land. Jesus is like a rock. Jesus was is and as always been. Jesus does not change. Jesus is like a solid stable rock that never moves and never changes. He is always safe to stand upon.

Salvation - Until Jesus comes and lives in our hearts we are lost in sin. (We must reach the age of accountability before we are lost in sin.) Salvations means we are saved by Grace through FAITH. We can not save our self. When the Holy Spirit draws us and we repent of our sins and ask Jesus into our hearts we receive salvation. Jesus becomes our Saviour.

The Great "I Am" – There is not greater explanation than he is "The great I am". He crated all things and in him is all power and glory. In God can all needs be meet. There is none great than the "I am". God almighty. God is an ever present (omni-present) God. The great I am is also know as: Messiah (John 4:26), Bread of Life (John 6:35), From above (John 8:23), Before Abraham (John 8:58), Light of the world, The door, Good Shepherd, Son of God, Resurrection and Life, Master, Way the truth and life, and true vine (John 15:1)

Valley – A valley is a time of our life when we are going through a very difficult time. Jesus is the Lily of the valley and he promised to be there for us and with us.

DID THIS BOOK TOUCH YOUR HEART?

THIS BOOK HAS BEEN A GREAT BLESSING TO ME! DID IT BLESS YOUR HEART? **DO YOU HAVE A TESTIMONY OF YOUR OWN?** WE WANT TO HEAR FROM YOU. WE HAVE PLANS FOR A VOLUME TWO OF THIS BOOK. WE WOULD LIKE TO HEAR YOUR TESTIMONIES AND STORIES. YOU NEVER KNOW WHO MAY BE TOUCHED BY YOUR STORY. THE ONLY REQUIREMENT IS THAT ANY AND ALL BIBLE

REFERENCES ARE TO THE KING JAMES VERSION BIBLE.
PLEASE SEND LETTERS TO:
**FAITH CHARITIES, P O BOX 5026, KNOXVILLE TN 37928
OR**
writteninFAITH@netscape.com

GOD BLESS YOU ALL!

Printed in the United States
65239LVS00007B/304-324

9 781600 342318